A Brief Descri
Whole \

George Abbot

Edited by:

Anthony Richmond

Goldenford Publishers Ltd
Guildford
www.goldenford.co.uk

First published in Great Britain in 2011 by
Goldenford Publishers Limited
The Old Post Office
130 Epsom Road Guildford
Surrey GU1 2PX
Tel: 01483 563307
Fax: 01483 829074
www.goldenford.co.uk

Cover design by Penelope Cline

Printed and bound by CPI Antony Rowe, Chippenham and Eastbourne

ISBN 978-0-9559415-2-8

Introduction

George Abbot was a Guildford man, through and through. He was born at one end of its High Street in 1562 and went on to receive his academic grounding at the Royal Grammar School, at the other end of the High Street. He went on to excel at Oxford and became one of the leading figures in the national scene but we know from his own words and actions that he never forgot the small world in which he started out.

He was aged 37 and Master of University College when in 1599 the 1st edition of his *Brief Description* was published. Abbot went on to play a significant part in the translation of the King James Bible, and in the same year as this was completed, 1611, he was made Archbishop of Canterbury.

His wealth and influence gave him the means to do some charitable work, and he found his "affection leading me to the Town of Guildford, where I was born, and where my aged Parents lived many years with good report". In 1619 he laid the foundation stone of his almshouse, the Hospital of the Blessed Trinity, which, as Abbot's Hospital, occupies such a prominent position in the High Street. This has survived nearly 400 years, though his other foundation, the *Manufacture,* designed to help workers suffering from the declining woollen trade by introducing the production of linen, was to last for only a few years.

The *Brief Description* is sometimes described as an early geography textbook, but readers will see that it is much more than this, and gives us a revealing glimpse of how a leading and forthright academic and churchman of this time regarded his world. His ideas of the world came entirely from his reading, at a time when most of human knowledge was thought to be accessible from the writings of others rather than through direct experience.

Although maps were becoming more easily available, he included none in his guide.

To us Abbot's *"Whole World"* may seem very small, because vast tracts of the globe were still to be discovered by western Europeans. In another way it was perhaps much bigger than ours, if we think of distance as a measure of time as much as of length.

In 1620 it took the *Mayflower* some 86 days to travel from Plymouth to the New World, and nearly a century later, we know from the need to hold the Duke of Monmouth in captivity overnight in Abbot's Hospital in 1685 that it took more than a day to ride from the New Forest to London, a little under 100 miles.

Another way in which Abbot's world was of a size unimaginable to us is that it was filled with strange and sometimes terrifying possibilities. The advance of science and discovery has told us that most of these are mere fantasies, leaving us with a more secure but much smaller world.

This edition is designed to be accessible to readers of today while still keeping the flavour of George Abbot's work. It has involved some translation, some modernising of words, spellings and typography, the provision of explanatory notes and the deletion of redundancies and ramblings. I have also deleted some, but in the interest of historical context, not all, comments which would today be found offensive, and I have rewritten many sentences; Abbot used copious semi-colons where we would use commas or full stops. There are still some very long sentences, but even these should now give the reader a chance to draw breath.

Abbot's work went into many subsequent editions. I have relied mainly on a 1634 edition in the possession of the Hospital, but have also used a facsimile of the 1608 edition at Lambeth Palace Library; this was procured with the help of a generous donation from the Royal Grammar School, Guildford, of which Abbot is an old boy.

My thanks are due to Sue Surridge, who performed so well the very difficult task of copying 17th century print into editable text, and to the History Department, both staff and students, of George

Abbot School, Guildford, for their kindness in looking over a late draft.

Above all I am grateful for the support and encouragement of the Governors of Abbot's Hospital, and to the residents who have made my work here in George Abbot's foundation such a rewarding experience.

Anthony Richmond
Abbot's Hospital, Guildford   April 2011
                                        www.abbotshospital.org

A Brief Description of

the Whole World

Wherein is particularly described all the Monarchies, Empires and
Kingdoms of the same, with their Academies

As also their several Titles and Situations thereunto adjoining

---

Written by the Right Reverend Father in God, George,
late Archbishop of Canterbury

London,

Printed for William Sheares, at the sign of
the Harrow in Britains Busse   1634

A Brief Description of the Whole World

The globe of the Earth shows either the sea or the land. The sea is the Ocean, which surrounds all the world, and takes its name either from the place near which it comes, as Persian Gulf, or from the finder out, as the Straits of Magellan; or of some other accident, as the Red Sea, because the sand is red.

There are some few seas which do not meet with the Ocean, such as the Dead Sea, near Palestine, the Caspian Sea, not far from Armenia: and such a one is said to be in the north part of America.

There are also the straits or narrow seas, such as the English Channel, the Straits between the Barbary Coast and Spain, and the Straits of Magellan.

The Earth is either islands, which are those which are wholly encompassed by the sea, such as Britain, or the continents, which are called in the English the firm land.

The old known continents are Asia, Europe and Africa. Europe is divided from Africa by the Mediterranean Sea and from Asia by the River Don. The north parts of Asia and Europe were but little known and discovered in old time.

Africa is divided from Europe by the Mediterranean Sea; from Asia, by the river Nile: and so Asia by the Don and Nile is severed from Europe and Africa.

Of Spain

To say nothing of England and Ireland, the most western country of Europe is Spain, which is bounded on the south with the Mediterranean, on the west with the Atlantic, on the north with the Bay of Biscay, or the Spanish seas, on the east with France, from which it is severed by the Pyrenees.

If we should enquire into the times that were before the coming of the Carthaginians and Romans into Spain, we shall find nothing but that which is either fabulous, or near to fables. It was first called Iberia, from the river Ebro, and afterwards Hispania.

It is certain that the Syrians planted a colony there in the isle of Gades, corruptly now called Cadiz. These, troubled by their neighbours, desired aid of the Carthaginians, who sent to defend them against their neighbours. Afterwards, heartened on by their success in their first expedition, these Carthaginians, successively sent thither three captains, Hamilcar, Hasdrubal and Hannibal, who for the most part subdued the province and held it, till by Scipio and the Roman forces, they were dispossessed of it.

Yet for many years after, the fortunes of the Romans stuck as it were in the subduing of that province, so that from the time of the second Punic war, until the time of Augustus, neither could they till that country nor bring it peacefully into the form of a province.

It continued a province of the Roman Empire until the time of Honorius the Emperor, in whose days the Vandals came into it, conquering and making it theirs.

Then the Goths (the Vandals either driven out, or called over into Africa) entering, erected there a kingdom, which flourished for many years, until by the coming of the Saracens and Moors, their kingdom was broken. Who, settling themselves in Spain, erected a kingdom, changed the names of many places and rivers, and gave them new names, such as they retain to this day, and

2

continued for the space of some hundreds of years mighty in that country, till they were first subdued by Ferdinand: afterwards, and that now lately [1609-1614], utterly expelled by Philip III.

After the coming in of these Africans, in this country there were many kingdoms, as the kingdom of Portugal toward the west; the kingdom of Granada toward the south; the kingdom of Navarre and Aragon toward the east; and the kingdom of Castile in the middle of the land: but the whole Dominion is now under the king of Spain.

There were in times past twelve separate kingdoms in Spain: old and new Castile, León, Aragon, Portugal, Navarre, Granada, Valencia, Toledo, Galicia, the Algarve, Murcia, and Cordoba. Which is not be wondered at, since in England, a far less country, there were in the time of the Saxons seven several kingdoms and monarchies.

In the best maps of Spain, the arms of these several kingdoms do yet distinctly appear, where for the arms of León is given a lion and for the arms of Castile is given a castle. Which was the cause that John of Gaunt, son to Edward III, king of England, did quarter with the arms of England the castle and the lion, as having married Constance, daughter to Peter king of Castile; and at this day the first and chief arms of the King of Spain, is a castle quartered with a lion, in remembrance of the two kingdoms of Castile and León.

In Cordoba (as in times past it was called) standeth Andalusia, near to which is the island called once Gades, but since, Cadiz, which was lately surprised by the English[1].

The kingdom of Granada, which lies nearest to the Mediterranean, was for 700 years possessed by the Moors and Saracens, who confess the religion of Mahomet.

The reason is shown by Rodericus Toletanus [Rodrigo Jiménez de Rada, 1170-1247, Archbishop of Toledo] to be this; that whereas

---

[1] Raided by Sir Francis Drake in 1587, delaying by a year the Spanish Armada, and in 1596 by the Earl of Essex – father of the third Earl, whose marital capacity was to play such an important part in George Abbot's relations with James I.

the Saracens after Mahomet's time, had spread themselves all along Africa, even into the western part of Barbary, a king of Spain called Rodrigo, employed as an ambassador to them one Don Julian, a nobleman, who by his wife's demeanour procured much reputation amongst the Moors. During his service, the king deflowered the daughter of the said Julian, which the Father took in such indignation, that he procured those Saracens to come over into Spain, that so he might be revenged on his king. But when those barbarous people had once set foot in there, they could never be removed, until the time of Ferdinand and Isabella, king and Queen of Spain, about 100 years since [1492].

Rodericus wrote, that before the coming of those Moors into Spain, King Rodrigo opened a part of a Palace which had been shut long before, and had by descent from hand to hand been forbidden to be entered by any. Yet the king supposed there had been great treasure there, and broke into it, but found nothing save, in a great chest, the pictures of men, who resembled the proportion, attire, and armour of the Moors, and a prophecy, that at that time when the Palace should be entered, such a people as were there shown, should invade and despoil Spain; which fell out accordingly.

The Spaniards are now a very mixed people, descended of the Goths, which in times possessed that land, and of those Saracens and Jews, which are the basest people of the world.

The kingdom of Portugal did contain under it the Algarve, but both of them are now annexed into Castile, by the coming of king Philip II of Spain [from 1556 to 1598], who took the advantage after the death of Sebastian, who was slain in Barbary in the year 1578. Then after him reigned Henry, who was a Cardinal, and uncle to Sebastian; in whose time, although show was made that it should be lawfully debated, to whom the Crown of Portugal did belong, yet [in 1580, after Cardinal-King Henry had died] Philip meaning to make sure work, did not so much respect the right, as by main force invaded, and since (to the great grief of the Portuguese) has kept it.

The chief city of Portugal is Lisbon from where those navigations were advanced, by which the Portuguese discovered so much of their south part of Africa and of the East Indies, which are possessed by them to this day. The city from where the Castilians set forth their ships to the West Indies is Seville. Another great city in Spain is Toledo, where the Archbishop is the richest spiritual dignity of Christendom, the Papacy only excepted.

In the last century there were reckoned to be in Spain, 4 archbishoprics of great worth, 3 other inferior, and 40 bishoprics; as also in Portugal, 3 archbishoprics and 8 bishoprics. There were also in Spain (besides the great officers of the Crown) 17 dukes, 41 marquesses, 87 earls or counts, and 9 viscounts: as also in Portugal (besides the officers of the Crown) 6 dukes, 4 marquesses, 19 earls, and 1 viscount. In Spain there are 7 universities.

The country is but dry, and so consequently barren, in comparison of some other places.

Not only this great and large country, once divided into so many kingdoms, is now under one absolute king, but that king also is lord of many other territories, such as the kingdom of Naples and the duchy of Milan in Italy, the isles of Sicily, Sardinia, Majorca, Minorca, Corsica, in the Mediterranean Sea, the islands of the Canaries in the Atlantic, besides various strong towns and good havens in Barbary, within and without the Straits.

On the backside of Africa he commands much on the frontier, besides the islands adjoining to the mainland. In the western Indies he has Mexico, Peru, Brazil, large territories, with the islands of the south and North Sea.

And Philip II getting Portugal as a dowry to that forc't marriage, got also all the dependencies of that Crown, in Africa, the east Indies, and the Atlantic Sea; the towns of Barbary and the east Indies willingly submitting themselves to him, but the Azores he won by force [in 1583] at the first and second expedition: so if we consider the huge tract of ground that is under this king's dominion, we will say that the empire of the King of Spain is in that respect the largest that now is, or ever was, in the world.

Of France

The next country is France, which is bounded on the west with the Pyrenees, on the north with the English seas, on the east with Germany, on the south east with the Alps, on the south west with the Mediterranean Sea.

The kingdom of France is one of the most rich and absolute Monarchies of the world, having both on the north and south side the sea, standing very convenient for profit of navigation, and the land itself being very fruitful.

The consideration whereof caused Francis I [1515-1547] to compare this kingdom alone to all the dominions and seigniories of the Emperor Charles V [1519-1556]: for when the herald of the said Charles, bidding defiance to King Francis, did give his Majesty the title of Emperor of Germany, King of Castile, Aragon, Naples, Sicily etc, Francis commanded his herald to call him King of France, as often as the other had titles by all his countries; implying that France alone was of as much strength and worth, as all the countries which the other had.

In the days of Francis II and Charles IX[2] there were three civil wars, which much ruined the glory and beauty of that kingdom, and a little before the great massacre in the year 1572[3], there had been peace in that country scarcely full two years, yet so great is the riches and happiness of that kingdom, that in that short time, all things were renewed and repaired again, as if there had never been any such desolation.

The revenue of the Crown of France is exceeding great, by reason of the taxes and impositions, which through the whole

---

[2] Francis II, 1559-1560, husband of Mary Queen of Scots; Charles IX, 1560-1574.
[3] St. Bartholomew's Day Massacre, in which several thousand French Protestants were killed.

kingdom are laid upon the subjects: for their sizes and totals exceed all imposts and tributes of all the Princes of Christendom; for there are few things there used, but the king turns them to his advantage; and not only with luxuries, as in other states, but with necessities, such as flesh, wood, salt, etc. It is supposed at this day, that there are in the kingdom 30,000 men, who are under-officers, and make a good part of their living by gathering of the king's tribute.

This is much increased no doubt in these latter times; but yet of old it was in so great measure, that the Emperor Maximilian said that the Emperor of Germany was king of kings, meaning that his Princes were such great men; the King of Spain was king of Men, because his people would obey their Prince in any reasonable moderation. The King of England was the king of Devils because the subjects had there several times deprived their kings of their crowns and dignity: but the King of France was king of Givers, in as much as his people did bear very heavy burdens of taxes and impositions.

In this kingdom of France is one great misery to the subjects, that the places and offices of justice are ordinarily bought and sold, the beginning of which was this. Louis XII, who was called a Father of the country, wished to pay the debts of his predecessor Charles VII[4] (which were very great) and intending to recover to France the dukedom of Milan, and minding not to burden his people further than was needed, thought it a good course to set at sale all the offices of the Crown. But with the places of justice he did not meddle, though his successors took occasion to make great profit of them also.

By the customs of that country, the king of France has not that absolute power to recruit soldiers, as in England, and some other places of Christendom the princes have. But the manner is, that when the king wishes for any military service, he sends abroad his edicts, or causes in cities and good towns, the drum to be struck

---

[4] Louis XII, 1498-1515, Charles VII 1470-1498.

up, and whoever will voluntarily follow, he is enrolled.

However, he needs to recruit few soldiers, because the nobles and gentlemen of France, hold it as their duty, and highest honour, both to attend the king to the wars, and to meet their own expenses, for many months. The person of the king of France has in former time been reputed so sacred, that their people have regarded them as if they had been demi-gods.

Machiavel[5] in his *Questions upon Livy,* says that they doted so upon their kings, that they thought everything they did was just right, and that nothing could be more disgraceful, than to suggest that anything was not well done by their king. But this opinion is not now much held. The Princes of the Blood [those legitimately descended in the male line from the monarch] are in the next rank under the king himself.

There are many very rich and goodly cities in France, but the chiefest of all is Paris: which place is especially honoured, first by the presence of the king, most commonly keeping court and residence there; secondly, by the great store of goodly houses, where part belong to noblemen, and part are houses of religion; thirdly, by the University, which is incomparably the greatest, most ancient, and best filled of all France; fourthly, in that it is the chief Parliament city of that kingdom, without the ratification of which Parliament at Paris, edicts and proclamations coming from the king, are not valid; fifthly, by the great traffic of all kind of merchandise, which is used in that place.

There are several cities in which provincial parliaments are held, and to these parliaments may be brought appeals from lower courts, but the Parliament of Paris has the right to hear appeals from all courts of the kingdom. That which we call our Parliament in England, is by them termed the States-General.

France in ancient time (as Caesar reports in the first of his

---

[5] Niccolò Machiavelli (1469-1527), Florentine civil servant, author of The Prince and of the Discourses on Livy.

Commentaries[6]) was divided into three parts: Aquitania, which was towards the west; Celtica, towards the north and west; and Belgica, which is towards the north. Belgica we commonly call the Low Countries: the government of the day is not at all under France, but Celtica and Aquitania are under the French king.

The ancient inhabitants of this country were the Gauls, who possessed not only all that we now call France, being the greatest part of that the Romans called Transalpine Gaul, but also a good part of Italy, which they call Cisalpine Gaul, a people whose beginnings are unknown. This of them is certain, that they were a nation of valour; for they not only sacked Rome, but also carried their conquering armies into Greece, where they settled down, and were called by the name of Galatians.

Some report also that they entered into Spain, and subdued and inhabited that part which was called Lusitania, now Portugal, but howsoever their former victories and greatness, they were by Julius Caesar subdued, made a province of the people of Rome, and so continued under the Roman empire until about 400 years after Christ, when in the ruin and dismembering of the Roman empire the French invaded Gaul, and erected a Monarchy. This has continued to this day in the succession of 64 kings, of three several races, that is to say, the Merovingians, Carolingians, and Capetians, about 1200 years, and now flourishes under Louis XIII,[7] the reigning King of France.

Although the French have done many things worthily out of their own country, in the east against the Saracens, and although they have for a while held Sicily, the kingdom of Naples, and the duchy of Milan, yet it hath been observed of them, that they could never make good their footing beyond the Alps, or in other foreign regions. However in itself France is one of the strongest kingdoms

---

[6] De Bello Gallico, the first words of which are *Gallia est omnis divisa in partes tres* = all Gaul is divided into three parts".

[7] Ruled 1601-1643, with the help of Cardinal Richelieu and the support of the (real) M. d'Artagnan, Lieutenant Captain of the first company of the king's Musketeers.

in all Europe at this day.

That which we commonly call the Low Countries, contains 17 provinces, which have several titles and governors, as the Dukedom of Brabant, the Earldom of Flanders, etc. The inheritance of these sometimes fell on daughters, who being married to the heirs of some of the other provinces, did in the end bring the whole country into one entire government, which was commonly called the Dukedom of Burgundy.

Yet in the union of them together, it was agreed that each of the provinces should retain their own ancient laws and liberties. This is the reason why some of those provinces in our age think themselves freed from obedience to the King of Spain. They came to him by inheritance, but he had violated their liberties, to the keeping whereof he was bound.

When the whole country belonged to the crown of France, the dukedom of Burgundy was bestowed by Philip de Valois King of France, to John de Valois a younger son of his[8], from whom by descent it came at last to Charles the Bold, otherwise the Proud, Duke of Burgundy, who left one only daughter. She was married to Maximilian the Emperor, of the house of Austria, from whom the inheritance descended to Charles V, Emperor, who, yielding it over to his son Philip II did charge him to treat that people well; which he forgetting to do, under pretence of rooting out the profession of religion, did entangle himself, and all that country with a very long, bloody and wearisome war.

There is no part of Europe which for the quantity of the ground, yields so much riches and commodity, as the Low Countries, besides their infinite store of shipping, wherein they exceed any prince of Christendom. They were in time past accounted a very heavy dull people, and unfit for the wars, but their continual

---

[8] Philip VI, 1328-1350, known, surprisingly, as "the Fortunate", in whose reign began the Hundred Years' War with England, in which he lost Calais and met a crushing defeat at Crécy. John II, the oldest of his seven children, was captured at Poitiers, and died in London.

combat with the Spaniards has made them now very ingenious, full of action, and managers of great causes appertaining to fights, either by sea or land. The seventeen provinces are Brabant, Gelderland, Artois, Valencois, Luxembourg, Flanders, Hainault, Lille, Namur, Holland, Zealand, Tournai, Liège, Mechelen, Utrecht, and the east and west Friesland.

France has many petty governments that do border upon it, such as the dukedom of Savoy, the state of the Switzers, the dukedom of Lorraine, the Burgundians or the Walloons, against all of which, the king is forced to keep his frontier towns.

There is nothing more famous in this kingdom, than the Salic Law, whereby it is provided, that no woman, nor the heir of her (as in her right) shall enjoy the crown of France, but it goes always to the heir male. It is said to be a great blessing of God, that they have the Salic law in France; not so much because women by the infirmity of their sex are unfit to govern, for therein many men who have enjoyed kingdoms, have been, and are very defective, but because by that means the Crown of France is never endangered by marriage of a foreigner, to come under the subjection of a stranger.

This Law is very ancient among them, so that it cannot certainly be defined when it was enacted: but by virtue of it Edward III, King of England, and his heirs were cut off from inheriting the Crown of France, whereto by marriage of a daughter he was heir in general.

And by reasons of this Law, Henry IV, late King of France, rather enjoyed that dominion, than the son of the Duke of Lorraine, who was nearer of blood by descending from the elder daughter of King Henry II.

The Switzers are a people called in old time Helvetii, who have no noblemen, or gentlemen among them, but only the citizens of their towns, the yearly officers and their Council, do govern their state.

There are in Switzerland 23 cities or towns, which they call their Cantons, although some rather think that name properly does signify the ruler of those towns; and of them some do retain to this day the Romish religion, but some others have embraced the Gospel. The country where they live, is not very fertile: and being far from any seas, they have no vent for their people, but by sending them forth as hired soldiers, which for their pay do fight often in Italy and France, and sometimes in Germany.

Near to one part of them stands Geneva, which is challenged by the Duke of Savoy, to have once belonged to his dominion: but they pretend themselves to be a free city, and by the help of Protestant Princes, but especially by some of the Helvetians, do so maintain it.

In this place there is a rare law, that if any malefactor, who has fled out of his own country, be convicted of any grievous crime, he suffer there, as if he were in his own country: which they are forced to do, because their city would be full of all sorts of runagates, in as much as they are close neighbours to several different princes and states.

Of Germany

The next country to France on the east side, is Germany, which is bounded on the west with France, and the Low Countries; on the north with Denmark, and the Danish seas; on the east, with Prussia, Polonia and Hungary; on the south-east, with Istria and Illyricum; on the south with the Alps and with Italy.

The governor of this country is called the Emperor of Germany [Holy Roman Emperor], who is chosen by three spiritual Princes, the Archbishops of Cologne, Mainz and Trier, and three temporal Princes, the Duke of Saxony, the Margrave of Brandenburg and the Count Palatine of the Rhine. If a majority cannot agree to an election, then the King of Bohemia has also a voice, so it comes to be said that there are seven Prince Electors of the empire.

The manner of the choice of the Emperor was established by a decree, commonly called The Golden Bull [1356] which was made by Charles IV and sets down all the circumstances of the election of the Emperor. He appoints the King of Bohemia to be Cup-Bearer, the three Archbishops to be Arch-Chancellors of the three several parts of the empire; the Count Palatine of the Rhine, to be Arch-Steward; the Duke of Saxony, to be Arch-Marshal, whose office it is to bear the sword; and the Margrave of Brandenburg, to be Great Chamberlain; all which offices they supply on the day of the Emperor's Coronation.

It appears by all the Roman stories that in times past the Empire went sometimes by succession, as to the sons of Constantine, and Theodosius, sometimes by election, and that either by the Senate, or by soldiers, who oftentimes in mutiny did elect men unworthy, yet such as fitted their purpose.

But now of late, the Electors do choose some prince of Christendom who has otherwise a dominion of his own, who may help the Empire, and therein of late has appeared the great cunning of that which we call the House of Austria, whose greatest title 300 years ago was to be a mean Count of a mean place, namely the County of Hapsburg [now in the Swiss canton of Aargau]. But since that time, they have so planted and strengthened themselves, that there have been seven or eight Emperors lately of that family; but the Empire is not tied to them, as may appear by the possibility, which the Duke of Saxony and Francis I, King of France [1515-1547], had to ascend to that dignity.

When Charles V was chosen Emperor, one of the means whereby the possession has been continued to that house, has been the electing of someone to be *Rex Romanorum* [King of the Romans], whilst another of his family was Emperor, which Charles V effected in his lifetime for his brother Ferdinand, who afterwards succeeded him; and that has been the attempt of Albert, late Cardinal, and now Archduke of Austria[9], that he might be established in the hope of the Empire, during the life of his brother Rudolph II, now Emperor and King of Bohemia. King of the Romans is the title given to the person expected to become Emperor upon the death, resignation, or deposition of the current Emperor.

He who is now Emperor of Germany, is called Caesar, [Kaiser] or Roman Emperor, but very improperly, as the case is far different from that which was when the Roman Empire did flourish, for then, the territories thereof were very great, all under the rule of one man, unless it pleased him to associate to himself some other. But Theodosius [ruled the whole Empire 392-395] divided the empire into two sovereignties, which were called the East and West Empires, and made Constantinople to be the chief seat of Arcadius, one of his sons, and Rome to be the principal city of Honorius, the other. Which Western Empire continued in its glory but a while, for the Goths and Lombards, and other barbarous

---

[9] Albert VII, nephew of Philip II of Spain, made Cardinal (though never ordained as a priest) at the age of 18 and later becoming first Viceroy of Portugal, Grand Inquisitor for that country, and a leading organiser of the Spanish Armada.

people, did both overrun it, and as good as extinguished it. So it continued until the days of Charlemagne [Emperor of the Romans 800-814], who revived it again: but although there was some show of dominion belonging to him in Italy, yet his principal residence was in France, and his successors removed it into Germany: so that properly he is now Emperor of the Germans.

It was a great policy of the Bishops of Rome for the Emperor to leave Italy, and keep himself in Germany: for the Popes did not like to have a strong neighbour so near, who might at his pleasure chastise or depose them, if he saw fit. And the cunning of those Popes was such also, that they weakened the state of the Emperor exceeding much in Germany, by giving great exemptions to the Princes thereof.

The arms of the Emperor bear the Spread Eagle with two heads, denoting the East and West Empire: but, it is said, one of the heads is quite pulled off, and to be almost all feathers; and in the other head, although life remains, yet there is little spirit or vigour. It is said that to the Emperor of Germany belong three Crowns: one of silver, which signifies the Kingdom of Germany; a second of iron, for the Kingdom of Lombardy, and a third of gold, which is for the sacred Roman Empire.

In Germany all are in some way under the command of the Emperor, but most of the Princes are in fact absolute governors in their dominions, so that they have liberty of religion, make laws, raise soldiers, and stamp money with their own pictures, as absolute Princes. So does the Duke of Saxony, the Archbishop of Cologne, and the rest.

The Princes of Germany came to the great strength of theirs, by means of a base and inferior man[10], who aspiring to the Empire (whereof he was unworthy) was content to release to the Princes almost all of their service and duty; so that their subjection since that time, is little more than titular, yielding only very small

---

[10] Probably Ferdinand II (Emperor 1619-1637), in whose reign began the disastrous Thirty Years' War.

maintenance to the Empire, either in tribute, soldiers, or otherwise. Although they do come to the Diets and Parliaments held by the Emperor, yet that is as much for the safeguarding of themselves from the invasion of the Turk[11], who is not far from them, as for any other reason. They treat this as a contribution, rather than anything imposed on them by duty; yet there is in existence a book which sets out how the Princes and free cities are bound to maintain upon their own charge 3,842 horse, and 16,200 foot [cavalry and infantry], for the service of the Emperor, when he shall see cause. But what a trifle is that in respect of the strength of so huge a country?

The Princes themselves are so strong, many of them, that they dare encounter with any who attack them, insomuch that although Charles V was doubtless the greatest Emperor that had been from the days of Charlemagne, yet the Duke of Saxony and the Landgrave of Hesse, with some few cities which were confederate with them, did dare to oppose themselves against the said Charles, and entering the field with him, did often put him to great inconveniences. It is supposed by some that his inability to match those Princes was why he resigned the Empire to his brother Ferdinand.

The manner of Germany is, that the title of nobility which is in the father, is commonly imparted to all the sons, so that every son of a Duke of Saxony, is called Duke of Saxony, and every child of the Count of Mansfield is honoured by the name of Count or Countess of Mansfield: but the main property remains with the eldest, for keeping upright the dignity of the family.

There are also free states and cities, which have the same authority, as Augsburg, Frankfurt and others. The Germans may boast this above other more westerly nations of Europe, that they are an unmixed nation: for whereas the Lombards and Goths at several times have set down in Italy, and mixed themselves with

---

[11]"The Turk" was a name widely used in Western Europe for the Sultan or Emperor of the Ottoman Empire.

the people there, the Goths, Vandals and Saracens in Spain; the Franks in Gaul, or France, and the Normans also; the Saxons, Angles, Danes and Normans in Great Britain; the Germans have been free from such inundation and mixture.

Of Italy

On the south side of the Alps and Germany, lies Italy, stretching itself out at length toward the south and east. It has on the south side, the island of Sicily, on the east, that part of the Mediterranean called the Adriatic Sea which separates Italy from Greece, on the west side that part of the Mediterranean which is called the Tyrrhenian Sea and on the upper or more northern part of it, the Ligurian Sea.

This country is by some likened to a long leaf of a tree. It has in the middle of it, which goes all in length a mighty mountain range called the Apennines, which is likened to the spine of the back. Out of these hills spring several rivers, which run on both sides of it into the Adriatic and Tyrrhenian Seas.

As in other countries, so in Italy in times past, there were various peoples, and several provinces, like our shires in England and so there be at this day: but the main division of Italy, as in our age we do account it, is properly into four parts. The first is Lombardy, which lies to the north. The second is Tuscany, which bounds toward the Mediterranean Sea, which way the island Corsica lies. The third is the land of the Church, which is the territory of the Bishop of Rome, and contains in it that which is called the Romagna; the fourth is Naples; and in this division now is all Italy comprehended.

In Tuscany, the chief city and commander of all the rest, is Florence, where is supposed to be the best language of Italy, called the common Italian, and the most circumspect policy of all the governments of Christendom, which has much been increased since the time of Machiavel, who was Secretary or Recorder to that State. This was in times past a free city but of late by the policy of the family of the Medici, it is brought under the subjection of a Duke, who reigns as an absolute Prince; and by little and little; has so encroached on his own citizens and neighbours round about him, that he has gotten to be called, (and that not unworthily) "The great Duke of Tuscany".

A great part of the rising of the family of the Medici, which are now Dukes of Florence, may be ascribed to the cunning carriage of themselves; but it has been much advanced forward by their felicity, in having two Popes together of that house, which were Leo X and Clement VII[12], who by all means laboured to establish the government of their country upon their kindred.

Affinity was contracted by them with the kings of France, when Catherine de Medici [1519-1589], niece to Pope Clement VII was married to the younger son of Francis V. His elder brother dying, that younger came to be King of France, by the name of Henry II. In his time she laid the foundation of her aspiring, so that after his death, where she bore the name of the Queen Mother, she swayed all at her pleasure in France during the successive reign of her three sons, Francis II, Charles IX, and Henry III. In all which time, no doubt, she promoted Florence and the Florentines to her uttermost.

A good part of Italy, commonly called the land of the Church, is under the Bishop of Rome, which is where the Pope is a prince absolute, not only spiritual as elsewhere he claims, but also temporal, making laws, requiring tribute, raising soldiers, and executing justice as a monarch.

The Bishops of Rome do pretend that Constantine the Great did bestow upon them the city of Rome, together with other cities and towns nearby, and the domains of them all, to be the Patrimony of St. Peter, as they call it. But Valla[13] has displayed the falsehood of that pretence.

---

[12] Leo X, son of Lorenzo de' Medici, The Magnificent, was Pope from 1513 to his death in 1521, the last non-priest to be so elected; his nephew Clement VII, Pope from 1523 to 1534.

[13] Lorenzo Valla (1406-1457), Italian humanist, in 1540 showed that the "Donation of Constantine" could be dated by its Latin style to the 8th Century, a much later era.

In truth, the greatness of the Popes rose first through Phocas[14,] who, killing his master the Emperor of Rome, and being favoured by the Bishop of that see, did in recompense thereof, suffer the Bishop of Rome to be proclaimed Universal Bishop, and of likelihood gave unto him somewhat to maintain his estate. And afterward King Pepin of France, and Charlemagne his son, getting (by means of the said Bishop) the kingdom of France, and then the empire, did bestow good possessions upon the Papacy.

Since that time the Popes have had so much wit, as by destruction of the princes of Italy, by encroaching on the favour of others, the great monarchs of Europe, and by their wars and other devices, to keep and increase that land of the Church, which in our time is well enlarged by the policy of Clement VIII, late Pope, who has procured that the dukedom of Ferrara is or shall be shortly added to his dominion[15].

The chief residence of the Bishop of Rome is Rome itself, which was first founded by Romulus, and afterwards so increased by others, who succeeded him. It was built upon seven hills, and has been ruled by seven sorts of government: that is, kings, consuls, decemvirs, tribunes of the people, dictators, emperors and popes.They first encroached on the neighbours about them in all Italy, Sicily, and some of the islands, until at length Rome proved to be the lady and chief mistress of the world: whose incredible wealth and greatness in men, treasure, shipping, and armour, was so huge, that it did even sink under the wealth of itself. Whereupon after several civil wars, such as those between Marius and Sulla, Pompey and Caesar[16], it became at length one absolute

---

[14] Flavius Phocas, Byzantine Emperor (602-610), taking the throne from the Emperor Maurice. Supported by Pope Gregory I, he consistently favoured the Papacy.

[15] Clement VIII, Pope 1592-1605; in 1597 the Duke of Ferrara died childless, and the Pope managed to attach this stronghold of the Este family to the Papal States.

[16] Marius (157-86 BC), seven times Consul, defeated by Sulla (138-78 BC), Dictator of Rome, the only man ever to have attacked and occupied both Athens and Rome; Pompey the Great (106-48 BC) , sole Consul, defeated by his sometime father-in-law and fellow Triumvir Julius Caesar (100-44 BC), Consul and Dictator of Rome until his assassination.

and imperial government, the majesty whereof was afterward somewhat impaired by the building of Constantinople, which was erected, or rather enlarged by Constantine the Great, and called New Rome.

When the division was made between the East and West Empire, it received a greater blow; yet the main overthrow of it was, when the Goths and Vandals entered Italy, sacked it, and possessed it at their own pleasure; so that it was (for a time) almost quite forsaken, and had no inhabitants, until the Bishops of Rome did make means to gather together some to people it again. Since those times, a good part of the old buildings upon the Hills, has been quite decayed and ruinated, and what may now be called (in comparison of the old) new Rome, is built on a lower ground. In times past this was termed the Field of Mars, very near to the river Tiber, as too well appears by the sudden flooding of the Tiber; destroying and spoiling men, cattle, and houses, very lately to their great loss.

The Bishops of Rome sometimes for their pleasure or profit withdraw to Bologna, or some other towns of Italy. Once, they removed their court to Avignon, a city in France, standing near the Mediterranean Sea, and not far from Marseilles in Provence, where for the space of 70 years their absence so afflicted the city of Rome, for lack of trade (which is very great when the Pope is there) that the Italians to this day do remember that time by the name of the Captivity of Babylon. This continued (as appears by the Scripture) for 70 years.

Whoever looks at the description laid down by the Holy Ghost in the Revelation shall see, that the Whore of Babylon there mentioned [chapters 17 and 18], can be understood of no place, but the city of Rome.

In the south part of Italy lies the Kingdom of Naples, which is a country very rich, and full of all kind of pleasure, abundant in nobility; whereof comes to be said that proverb, "Naples for Nobility, Rome for Religion, Milan for Beauty, Florence for Policy, and Venice for Riches".

This was once heretofore ruled by a king of their own, until the time of Queen Joan of Naples [ruled 1414-1435], who by deed of gift, did first grant that kingdom to the kings of Aragon in Spain; and afterward by will, with a revocation of the former grant, did bequeath it to the house of Anjou in France. Since which time the Kingdom of Naples has sometimes been in the hands of the Spaniard, sometimes possessed by the French, and is now under the King of Spain: to this is annexed also the dukedom of Calabria.

This Kingdom of Naples lies so near to the part of Greece which is now in possession of the Turk, that it may justly be feared that at some time or other the said Turk should make invasion thereunto, as indeed he has threatened to do several times, and sometimes has landed men, to the great terror of all Italy. For the preventing of that mischief, the King of Spain is enforced to keep a good fleet of galleys continually at Otranto, where is the nearest passage from Italy into Greece.

This part of Italy was in times past was named *Magna Graecia* [Greater Greece], but in latter ages it has been improperly called one of the Sicilies, which was reproved long since by Aeneas Silvius[17] in his 12th Epistle; and yet until recently the Kings of Spain have been termed Kings of both the Sicilies.

There be moreover in Italy many other princedoms and states, such as the dukedoms of Ferrara, Mantua, Urbino, Parma and Piacenza, and the states of Lucca and of Genoa. These are governed by their Senate, but have a Duke as they have at Venice. There be also some other, by which means the glory and strength of Italy is decayed.

---

[17] Pius II, Pope, 1458-1464; scholar, before his election described as "frivolous" and "dissolute" (*Catholic Encyclopaedia*).

Of Denmark, Sweden, and Norway

As Italy lies on the south side of Germany, so Denmark lies on the north; into the middle of which land, the sea breaks in by a place called the Sound, the customs duties from which passage bring great riches to the King of Denmark. This is a kingdom, and ruled by an absolute governor.

On the north and east side of Denmark, lies Sweden, which is also a kingdom of itself: where the King professes himself to be *Rex Succorum, Gothorum, Vandalorum* [King of the Swedes, the Goths and the Vandals]. Whereby we may know that the Goths and Vandals, which in times past did waste Italy, and other nations of Christendom, did come out of this country.

This whole area which contains in it Norway, Sweden and some part of Denmark is a Peninsula, being very much compassed about with the sea. This is it, which is termed Scandinavia: on the north and west side of Sweden, lies Norway, which is at this day under the government of the kingdom of Denmark, although heretofore it has been a free kingdom of itself.

Within the Sound, on the east part of the sea, lies Danzig [Gdansk] about which are the towns of the Hanseatic League[18], confederates and allies to the king of Denmark. These are very rich towns, by reason of merchandise which they receive down the rivers out of Poland and transport to other parts of Christendom, through the Sound of the King of Denmark. They live as free people, keeping amity with the Kings of Sweden and Denmark, and with the Emperor of Germany: but within these late years, Stephen Báthory, the King of Poland [1576-1586] has sought their allegiance and by war forced them to capitulate with him.

---

[18] An alliance of cities in northern Europe, dominating trade along that coast in the 13th to 17th centuries.

There is no great thing to be noted in these countries, but that from Denmark comes much corn, to the supply of other parts of Christendom, and that from all these countries, is brought great furniture for war, or for shipping; as masts, cables, steel, saddles, armour, gunpowder, and the like. In the seas adjoining to these parts, there are fishes of much more monstrous shape than elsewhere are to be found. The people of those countries are by their profession Lutherans for Religion.

Of Russia, or Muscovy

On the east side of Sweden begins the dominion of the Emperor of Russia, although Russia, or Muscovy itself, does lie somewhat more into the east. It is a great and mighty monarchy, extending itself even from Lapland and Finland, many thousand miles in length, to the Caspian Sea: so that it contains in it a great part of Europe, and much of Asia also.

The governor there calls himself Emperor of Russia, Great Duke of Muscovy and many other titles of princedoms and cities. His dominion was very much enlarged by the Emperor not long since dead, Ivan IV, who reigning long, and being fortunate in war, did very much enlarge this mighty dominion.

This man in his younger days was very fortunate, and added very much to the glory of his ancestors, winning something from the Tartars, and something from the Christians in Livonia, Lithuania, and other bordering countries. In his latter age, growing more unwieldy, and less beloved of his subjects, he proved as unfortunate[19]. Whereby it came to pass, that Stephen Báthory won from him large provinces, which he before had conquered.

Gregory XIII, Bishop of Rome[20], thinking by his entreaty for peace between those two princes to have won the whole Russian Monarchy to the subjection and acknowledgement of the papacy,

---

[19] Tsar Ivan IV Vasilyevich, ruled from 1533, at the age of three, to 1584; known in England as Ivan the Terrible. During his reign Russia expanded to include Siberia and other Tartar regions. Apparently prone to great rages and perhaps mental instability; in his last years he is said to have sought to leave Moscow and seek asylum in England. Ivan was much admired by Josef Stalin.

[20] Gregory XIII, Pope 1572-1585, gave his support and name to the Gregorian calendar; encouraged plans of Philip II of Spain for the assassination or dethroning of Elizabeth I of England.

sent Robertus Possevinus[21] a Jesuit, (but yet a great statesman) as his agent to take up the controversies, between the Muscovite and the King of Poland.

He prevailed so far that he drew them to tolerable conditions for both parties; but when he began to exhort the Emperor to accept the Romish faith, he utterly and with much scorn rejected all obedience to him, having been informed by the English Ambassador (whom he very much favoured for the sake of his Lady and Mistress Queen Elizabeth sake) that the Bishop of Rome was a proud prelate, and would exercise his pretended authority so far, as to make kings and Princes hold his stirrup, and even to kiss his feet.

Possevinus replied that although the princes of Europe did indeed offer to kiss his feet, in acknowledgement of their subjection to him, as the Vicar of Christ and successor of Saint Peter, the Pope, remembering himself to be a mortal man, did not take that honour as due to himself; he had on his slipper a picture of Christ, hanging upon the Cross, and in truth he would have the reverence done thereunto.

The Tsar did grow into an exceeding rage, saying that his pride was so much the greater if he put the Crucifix upon his shoe; for Russians hold, that so holy a thing as that is highly profaned, if any resemblance of it be worn.

Possevinus, in a treatise written of his embassy to that country, where he mentioned this whole matter, confessed, that he was much afraid lest the Emperor would have stricken him, and beaten out of his brains with a pointed staff which then he had in his hands, and did ordinarily carry with him.

He had the more reason so to fear, because that Prince was such a tyrant, that he had slain, and with cruel torture put to death very many of his subjects, and members of the nobility, showing himself

---

[21] In fact Antonius Possevinus, 1534-1611, an Italian priest who acted as papal legate.

more brutishly cruel to them, than ever Nero or Caligula[22] were among the Romans.

Not only this but he had with his own hands, and with the same staff, upon a small occasion of anger, killed his eldest son, who should have succeeded him in his empire[23].

The people of this country, are rude and unlearned, so that there is very little or no knowledge amongst them of any letters; yes, their very priests and monks (whereof they have many) are almost unlettered, so that they can hardly do anything more than read their ordinary service.

The rest of the people are, by reason of their ignorant education, dull and incapable of any high understanding, but very superstitious, having many ceremonies, and idolatrous solemnities, such as the consecrating of their rivers by their Patriarch at one time of the year, when they think themselves much sanctified by the receiving of those hallowed waters and even bathe their horses and cattle in them.

Also they bury most of their people with a pair of shoes on their feet, supposing that they have a long journey to go, and with a letter in their hand to S. Nicholas, whom they reverence as a special Saint, and think that he may give them readier admission into heaven.

The Muscovites have received the Christian Faith but they rather hold of the Greek, and the eastern, than of the western Roman Church.

The doctrines wherein the Greek Church differs from the Latin, are these: first, they hold that the Holy Ghost proceeds from the Father alone, and not from the Son; secondly, that the Bishop of Rome is not the universal Bishop. Thirdly, that there is no Purgatory, fourthly, their priests do marry, fifthly, they do differ in

---

[22] Roman emperors of the 1st century AD, both renowned for egocentricity and casual cruelty.

[23] In 1581, Ivan hit his pregnant daughter-in-law for wearing what he took to be immodest clothing, and this may have brought about a miscarriage. His son remonstrated with him, and was struck about the head in what proved a fatal blow.

divers of their ceremonies, as in having four Lents in the year, whereof they do call our Lent, their great Lent.

At the time of the Council of Florence[24], there was some show made by the agents of the Greek Church, that they would have joined in opinion with the Roman Church: but when they returned home, their countrymen would in no sort assent thereunto.

In the northern parts of the dominion of the Emperor of Russia, which have lately been joined to his territories, as specially Lapland, Biarmia[25], and thereabouts, there are people so rude and heathenish, that (as Olaus Magnus writes of them) whatsoever living thing they do see in the morning at their going out of their doors, yes, if it be a bird, or a worm, or some such other creeping thing, they do yield a divine worship, and reverence thereunto for all that day, as if it were some inferior god.

The greatest part of the country of Russia is in the winter so exceeding cold, that the rivers are frozen over, the land covered with snow, and such is the sharpness of the air, that if any go abroad bare faced, it causes their flesh in a short time to rot, which befalls to the fingers and toes of divers of them. Therefore for a great part of winter, they live in stoves and hothouses: and if they have to go abroad they use many furs, whereof there is great plenty in that country, as also wood to make fire.

But yet in the summer time, the face of the soil, and the air is very strangely altered, insomuch that the country seems hot, the birds sing very merrily, and the trees, grass, and corn, in a short space do appear so cheerfully, green, and pleasant, that it is scant to be believed, but by them which have seen it.

Their building is most of wood, even in their chief city of Moscow, insomuch, that the Tartars (who lie in the north east of them, breaking often into their countries, even to the very

---

[24] A Council of the Church held between 1431 and 1445. The agreements reached with the Orthodox Church were finally made void by the fall of Constantinople to the Turks in 1453.
[25] Southern shores of the White Sea and the basin of the Northern Dvina River, now known as the Oblast of Archangel.

Moscow), do set fire on their cities, which by reason of their wooden buildings, are quickly destroyed.

The manner of government which of late years has been used in Russia is very barbarous, and little less than tyrannous: for the Emperor that last was, did suffer his people to be kept in great servility, and permitted the rulers and chief officers at their pleasure to pillage and ransack the common sort. But this was to no other end, but that he himself might take occasion (when he thought good) to call them in question for their misdemeanour, and so fill his own coffers with fleecing of them. Which was the same course the old Roman emperors did use, calling the deputies of their provinces by the name of sponges, whose property is to suck up water, but when it is full, then itself is crushed, and yielded forth liquor for the behalf of another.

The passage by sea into this country [through the White Sea and Archangel] was first discovered by the English, who with great danger of the frozen seas, did first adventure to sail so far north, as to compass Lapland and Finmark [extreme northeast of Norway] and so passing to the east by Novaya Zemlya, half the way almost to Cathay [China], have entered the river by which they disperse themselves for merchandise, both by water and land, into the most parts of the dominion of the Emperor of Russia.

The first attempt which was made by the English to sail to Muscovy by the north seas, was in the days of King Edward VI, at which time the Merchants of London procuring leave of the king did send forth Sir Hugh Willoughby, with shipping and men. He went far toward the north and turned toward the east: but the weather proved so extreme, the snowing so great, and the freezing of the water so vehement, that his ship was set fast in the ice, and there he and his people were frozen to death.

The next year some other coming from England, found both the ship and their bodies, in it, and a perfect remembrance in writing, of all things which they had done and discovered; where amongst the rest, mention was made of a land, which they had touched, which to this day is known by the name of Sir Hugh Willoughby's land[26].

The Merchants of London did not desist to pursue this discovery, but have so far prevailed, that they have reached one half of the way, toward the east part of China, and Cathay, but the whole passage[27] is not yet opened.

This empire is at this day, one of the greatest dominions in the world, both for compass of ground, and for multitude of men; saving that it lies far north, and so yields not pleasure or good traffic, with many other of the best situated nations.

Among other things which show the magnificence of the Emperor of Russia, this one is recorded by many, who have travelled into those parts; that when he sits in his magnificence, besides great store of jewels, abundance of massive plate both of gold and silver, which is openly showed in his hall, there sit also as his princes and great nobles men clothed in very rich and sumptuous attire, ancient yet very seemly of countenance, and grave, with white long beards, which is a goodly show.

But Olaus Magnus, a man well experienced in those northern parts, says (how truly I cannot tell) that this is a notable fraud and cunning of the Russian; inasmuch as they are not men of any worth, but ordinary citizens of the gravest and seemliest countenance, who for such solemn occasions are picked out of Moscow, and other places adjoining, and have robes put on them, which are not their own, but taken out of the Emperor's wardrobe.

---

[26] Now believed to be the western part of the two main islands of Novaya Zemlya.
[27] The north-east Passage, not fully navigated until 1878.

Of Prussia and Poland

In Europe, on the east and north corner of Germany, lies a country called Prussia, of which little is famous, save that they were governed by one, in a kind of order of religion[28], whom they call the Grand Master: and that they are a means to keep the Muscovite, and the Turks from some other parts of Christendom.

This country is now grown to be a dukedom, and the Duke there allows traffic with our English, who going beyond the Hanseatic towns, do touch upon his country; and amongst other things bring from there a kind of leather, which was wont to be used in jerkins.

Between Russia and Germany lies Poland, a kingdom differing from others in Europe because the king there is chosen by election from some of the princes near adjoining, as lately Henry III, King of France. These elections often make great factions there, which grow into civil war.

The King of Poland is almost continually at war, either with the Muscovites, who lie to the east and north east of him or with the Turk, who lies on the south and south east, and sometimes also with the princes of Germany. So the Poles commonly desire to choose warriors as their kings.

In this country are none but Christians, but liberty of all religion is permitted, and there are Papists, Colleges of Jesuits, Lutherans and Calvinists, Anabaptists, Aryans, and others.

But of late years, there have been motions in their parliaments, that their Colleges of Jesuits should be dissolved and that they should banished out of that kingdom, as of late they were from France. The reason is that under colour of religion, they do secretly

---

[28] The Teutonic Knights, a crusading military order, ruled what is now Prussia until the 15th century.

deal in state causes, and many times sow seditions, and some of them have given counsel to murder princes: and wheresoever they be, they are only intelligencers for the Pope.

Besides that, many of the Papists (but especially all their friars and orders of religion) do hate and envy them: first, because they take upon themselves with such pride to be called Jesuits, as if none had to do with Jesus but they, and because they are closer to princes than the rest are. Secondly, because many of them are more learned than common monks and friars, and thirdly, because they behave themselves more strictly and severely than others do, the Capuchins only excepted.

This is that country which in times past was called Sarmatia[29,] the chief city whereof is named Kraków.

---

[29] A poetic name for Poland; in antiquity the Sarmatians were tribes who lived to the north of the Black Sea, according to legend descended from Japheth son of Noah.

Of Hungary and Austria

On the south east side of Germany lies Hungary, an absolute kingdom, which has been heretofore rich and populous. The Christian population follows various forms of religion, as in Poland.

This kingdom has been a great obstacle against the Turks coming into Christendom; but especially in the time of János Hunyadi[30], who did mightily, with many great victories, repulse the Turk. Here stands Buda, which was heretofore a great fortress of Christendom: but the glory of this kingdom is almost utterly decayed, by reason that the Turk, who partly by policy and partly by force, does now possess the greatest part of it. So that the people are fled from there, and the Christians which remain there, are in miserable servitude. Notwithstanding some part of Hungary does yet belong to Christendom.

The Turks for the space of these 40 or 50 years last past, have kept continual garrisons, and many times great armies in that part of Hungary, which yet remains Christian.

Yes, and sometimes the Great Turks [Ottoman Emperors] themselves have come here in person with huge hosts, accounting it a matter of their religion, not only to destroy as many Christians as they can, but also to win their land, by the revenues whereof they may maintain some religious house, which they think themselves in custom bound to erect. But so that the maintaining thereof is by the sword to be won out of the hands of some of those whom they hold enemies to them.

Hungary is become the only cockpit [battlefield] of the world, where the Turks do strive to gain, and the Christians, supported by the Emperor of Germany (who entitles himself King of Hungary)

---

[30] Nicknamed The White Knight, Regent-Governor 1446–1453.

do labour to repulse them: and few summers do pass, but that something is either won or lost, by their party.

That corner of Germany which lies nearest to Hungary is called Austria, which is an archdukedom. From which house come many of the princes of Germany, and of other parts of Europe; so that the Crown Imperial of Germany has often fallen to someone of this house.

In this country stands Vienna, that noble city, which is now the principal bulwark of Christendom against the Turk from whence Suleiman[31] was repelled by Ferdinand [Archduke of Austria, Ferdinand I of Habsburg, king of Hungary 1526-1564, Holy Roman Emperor 1558-1564] in the time of the Emperor Charles V [1529]. It was in this country, that Richard I, King of England, on his return from the Holy land, was taken prisoner by the Archduke of Austria, and so put to a grievous ransom[32].

Rudolf II [Holy Roman Emperor 1576-1612] had several brothers, who were all called Archdukes of Austria, according to the manner of the Germans, who give the titles of the father's nobility to all the children. The names of them were Matthias, Ernest, and Albert, the youngest, who for a good space held by dispensation from the Pope, the Archbishopric of Toledo in Spain, although he was not a priest, and had then also the title of Cardinal of Austria and was employed as Viceroy of Portugal, by Philip II, king of Spain.

After the death of the Duke of Parma, he was sent as Lieutenant-General and Governor of the Low Countries, where he married the Infanta Isabella Eugenia Clara, eldest daughter to King Philip II, and by her had the title of Duke of Burgundy, although

---

[31] Known in the West as Suleiman the Magnificent, Sultan of the Ottoman Empire, 1520-1566.

[32] So giving rise to the legend of the minstrel Blondel, who is said to have found him by singing a song they both knew outside various castles and waiting for a reply, and adding a further string to the bow of the probably mythical Robin Hood, who is said to have safeguarded the ransom against the plots of Richard's brother Prince (later king) John.

peaceably he could not enjoy a great part of that country.

Throughout both Austria and Hungary runs the mighty River Danube, as throughout Germany does run the Rhine, whereon grows Rhenish wine.

Of Greece, Thrace, and countries near adjoining

On the south side of Hungary and southeast, lies a country of Europe, called in old time Dacia, which is large and wide, comprehending Transylvania, Wallachia, Moldavia, and Serbia. Of which little is famous, save that the men are warlike, and can hardly be brought to obedience. They have lately been under the king of Hungary.

These countries of Transylvania, Wallachia and Moldavia, have certain monarchs of their own, whom they call by the name of Voivode, which do rule their countries with indifferent mediocrity, while they have the sway in their own hands. But having the Turk as neighbour, they are many times oppressed and overcome by him, so that often they are his tributaries.

Yet by the wildness of the country, and uncertain disposition of the rulers and their people, he never has any hand over them for long. Sometimes they maintain war against him, and have slain some of his generals, coming with a great army against them; by which occasion it falls out, that he is glad now and then to enter confederacy with them: so doubtful a kind of rule is that in those countries nowadays.

The river Danube divides this Dacia from Bulgaria and Russia, which lies on the south of the river, and is separated from Greece by the Balkan mountains.

It was reported in times past, though but falsely, that those standing on the top of these hills might see the sea in all four directions, to wit, east, west, north and south. Under pretence of trying which conclusion, Philip, King of Macedonia (not Philip the father of Alexander, but a later) did go up to the hills, when in truth his meaning was secretly to meet with others there, with whom he might join himself against the Romans, which was shortly the overthrow of that kingdom. It seems that around here it is very cold, as shown by the jest concerning these hills, when it is said that for eight months in the year it was very cold, and for the other four, it was winter.

From the Balkans towards the south lies Greece, bounded on the west by the Adriatic Sea, on the east by the Thracian Sea, and the Aegean Sea; on the south by the main Mediterranean Sea.

This contained in old time four special parts, the Peloponnese, Achaea, Macedon and Epirus.

The Peloponnese is now called the Morea, in the southern part of Greece, being a peninsula or almost an island. Herein stood the ancient state of Sparta, or Lacedaemon, the laws whereof were made by Lycurgus. By the due observation of which, Cicero could say in his time, that Sparta had continued in the same ways and behaviour for the space of 700 years.

Sparta often made war against the Athenians, and this and Athens were called the two edges of Greece.

Near the Isthmus, or Straits, stood the famous city of Corinth, which was in old time called the Key of Greece, and where St Paul wrote two of his Epistles.

Aeneas Sylvius[33] in his cosmographical treatise *De Europa*, says that the Straits which divide Morea from the rest of Greece, are in breadth but five miles, and that various kings and princes did go about to dig away the earth, that they might make it to be an island. He names Julius Caesar, Caligula, and Nero, and notes that they not only failed of their purpose, but that they all came to violent and unnatural deaths.

From the Isthmus, which is the end of the Peloponnese, or Morea, begins Achaia, and spreads itself northward but a little way, to the boundary with Macedon: it extends eastward to the island of Euboea, with a great promontory, and westward bounding to Epirus.

---

[33] Pius II, Pope 1458-1464, a prolific author, whose works include an autobiography and his *The Tale of the Two Lovers*, an erotic novel which is said to be true to nature.

The inhabitants of this place were properly called Achivi; which word is so often used by Virgil. Here toward the east part stood Boetia, and upon the sea coast, looking southward toward Morea, was Athens, which was famous for the laws of Solon, for the wars against Sparta, and many other cities of Greece; and for a university of learned men, which long continued there[34].

In this part of Greece stood Parnassus and Helicon[35], so much talked of by the poets, and Phocis and Thebes.

The third province of Greece, called Epirus, lies to the west of Achaia, and extends itself for a good space that way; but toward the north and south it is but narrow, lying along the sea coast, and looking southward on the islands of Corfu and Cephalonia.

This was the country wherein Olympias, wife to Philip of Macedon, and mother to Alexander the Great, was born. This was also the kingdom of that noble Pyrrhus[36], who made such great wars against the Romans.

In our latter age it was made renowned, by the valiant Scanderbeg[37,] who was so great a scourge to the Turk, whose life is so excellently written [1508-1511] by Marin Barleti.

From the east part of Epirus northward, lies an area which had no famous name; but, it seems, was sometimes under Epirus, to which it lies northward, sometimes under Macedon, to which it lies westward, sometimes under Illyria, to which it lies southward. It may be that there were in old time some free cities there.

Illyria, which borders on Greece towards the north and west, near to the top of the Adriatic Sea, and not far from Venice, is

---

[34] The Academy, an area in which Plato taught from around 387 BC, and which remained in one form or another a centre of learning until AD 529.

[35] Both Mount Parnassus and Mount Helicon were in the Greek mythology homes of the Muses.

[36] One of the earliest (c. 280 BC) opponents of Rome; he won battles but suffered very heavy casualties, hence the phrase 'Pyrrhic victory', one which comes at too great a cost.

[37] 1405-1468; known as the Dragon of Albania, ousted the Turks for more than 20 years.

under the rule of that city.

The fourth and greatest part of old Greece was Macedon, which is falsely by the maps of the Roman empire, placed on the west of Greece; for in truth it lies on the east, looking toward Asia Minor, being bounded on the east by the Aegean, on the south by Achaia, and part of Epirus: and on the west, by certain great mountains; but on the north, by the Balkans.

This was the kingdom so famous in times past for Philip and Alexander his son, who conquered the whole world, and caused the name of the third empire to be attributed to this place. Here stood the hill Athos, whereof part was dug down by the army of Xerxes the great king of Persia, who warred against the Greeks [in 483 BC]. Here was Mount Olympus, and the city of Philippi, where the Philippians dwelt, to whom St Paul wrote. The whole country of Thessaly lies to the south of this part of Greece.

In this country of Greece, were in ancient time many kingdoms and states, as at this day there are in Italy; as the Macedonians, the kingdom of Epirus, the State of Athens, the government of Sparta, the city of Thebes, and very many other places; insomuch that almost every town had a peculiar government. But now it is all under one monarchy.

From Greece (in old time) did almost all famous things come. These were they that made the war against Troy; that resisted Xerxes the mighty king of Persia; that had the famous law-makers, as Solon in Athens, and Lycurgus in Lacedaemon; that rose against the rule of the Persians; that brought forth famous captains, such as Themistocles, Miltiades, Alexander, and many others that were the authors of civility to the western nations, and to some in Asia Minor: that gave to Italy and to the Romans the first light of learning, because from them arose the first poets, such as Homer, Hesiod, Sophocles, and others.

They were the cradle of the great philosophers, Socrates, Plato, Aristotle, together with Stoics, Peripatetics and Epicurians, and of the great orators Demosthenes and Eschines; and in one word (mathematics excepted, which came rather from the Chaldeans and the Egyptians) the whole flower of arts and good learning.

On the north east part of Greece stands Thrace, which heretofore has not been distinguished, is now accounted as the chief part of Greece. Here on the edge of the sea coast very near to Asia, stands the city called Byzantium, once Constantinople, because Constantine the Great did new build it, and made it an imperial city.

This was the chief residence of the Emperor of Greece, sometimes called New Rome, and the glory of the east; where the General Council was once assembled; and the see of the Patriarch of Constantinople. But by the great discord of the Christians, all Greece, and this city, are fallen into the hands of the Turk who now makes it his place of imperial abode. It was won in the time of Constantine the last Emperor; so that by Constantine it gained its honour, and by Constantine it lost it[38]. In this city is an Ambassador to the Turk for the King of England.

The Christians that do live now in Greece are in miserable servitude to the Turk. They disagree in many things from the doctrine of the Church of Rome.

---

[38] Constantinople was consecrated by Constantine the Great in 330 BC, and under Constantine XI fell to the Turks in AD1453.

Of the Sea running between Europe and Asia

If there were no other proof that the northern parts of the world were not discovered in times past, by any that travelled that way, yet this would sufficiently show it, that there was never thought to be any land between Asia and Europe, higher than the river Don, which does not extend itself very far into the north, but is short of the northern coast by the space of 4,000 miles. This river leaves Asia on the east side, and Europe on the west; but going southwards, it disburdens itself into a dead lake or fen (for so it seems) which is the Sea of Azov. In the dead of winter it is usually so frozen, that the Scythians and Tartars near adjoining, do both themselves and their cattle, yea sometimes with sleds after them, pass over, as if it were dry land.

On the southern part of this is a narrow strait of the sea, which is commonly called by the name of Cimmerian Bosporus. When this water has run for a pretty space, there begins a great and wide sea, named the Black Sea, where as it is said the whale did carry the Prophet Jonah, and there did disburden himself of his luggage by casting him upon the land.

At the mouth of this sea, is a very great strait, known by the name of the Bosphorus, with a breadth not above one mile, severing Asia and Europe. On the side of Europe stands Constantinople, on the side of Asia, the city called Pera, or Galata which is by some reckoned a part of Constantinople.

When any of the Emperor's janissaries[39] have done anything

---

[39] Janissaries were the elite soldiers of the Ottoman Empire, becoming in their formation in the middle of the 14th century the first European standing army since the days of Rome. Traditionally, conscripted from non-Turkish, often Christian, children, they formed the Emperor's bodyguard and in battle were used as shock troops.

worthy of death, the custom is, to send them by night over by boat from Constantinople to Pera. On the way he is thrown into the water, with a great stone about his neck, and then there a great gun is shot off, which is a token of some such execution. The Emperor is forced to take this course, lest the rest of his janissaries should mutiny when any of their fellows is put to death.

Constantinople is marvellously, richly, and conveniently situated, by reason of the standing of Asia and Europe so near together, with the sea running between them. This serves it with all manner of commodities, and it is therefore a fit place from which the Emperor may make great attempts.

After this strait, the sea opens itself more large toward the south, and it is called by the name of the Sea of Marmara. Then it grows again into another strait, which they write to be in breadth about two miles; this is called the Hellespont, having on the one side Abydos in Asia, and on the side of Europe Sestos. This is the place where Xerxes the Great, king of Persia, made his bridge over the sea, so much renowned in ancient History, the foundation of his bridge being rested on ships.

Here also is the place of the story of Leander and Hero: Leander is reported for the love of Hero, to have often swam over the sea, until at last he was drowned. From this strait southward, the sea grows more wide, and is called afterwards by the name of the Aegean Sea, and eventually the Mediterranean.

Of Asia, and first of Tartary

On the north side of Asia, joining to the dominion of the Emperor of Russia, is Tartary[40], in ancient time called Scythia[41]; the bounds whereof did then extend themselves into a good part of Europe: but the greatest part of it lies in Asia, a mighty large country, extending itself on the north to the uttermost sea[42], on the east to the dominion of the great Cham or Prince of Cathay [China]; on the south down to the Caspian Sea.

The Tartars which now inhabit it, are men of great stature, rude of behaviour, no Christians, neither do they acknowledge Mahomet. They have few or no cities among them, but after the manner of the old Scythians, do live in the wilderness, lying under their carts, and following their droves of cattle, by the milk whereof they do nourish themselves. They sow no corn at all, because they abide not long in any one place; but taking their direction from the northern pole star, they remove from one coast of their country to the other.

The country is populous, and the men are great warriors, fighting always on horseback with their bow and arrows, and a short sword. They have amongst them infinite store of horses, whereof they sell many into the countries near adjoining. Their ordinary food in their wars is horse flesh, which they eat raw, it

---

[40] European name given to a large area of northern and central Asia, including modern Siberia, Manchuria, Mongolia and Turkestan, between the Urals and the Caspian Sea and the Pacific.

[41] Scythia was a quite different area, including parts of modern Russia, the Ukraine, Kazakhstan and Azerbaijan.

[42] Presumably the Arctic Ocean – though Abbot will have been familiar with Psalm 139:9, in the 16th century translation by Myles Coverdale, "If I take the wings of the morning, and remain in the uttermost parts of the sea, even there also shall thy hand lead me, and thy right hand shall hold me".

being warmed a little by hanging at their saddle.

They have great wars with the countries adjoining, but especially with the Muscovites, and sometimes with the Turks.

From hence came Tamburlaine[43], who brought 700,000 of the Tartars at once into the field, wherein he distressed and took prisoner Bayezid the great Turk, whom he afterward forced to feed like a dog under his table.

They have amongst them many princes and governors. The Crimean Tartars have one, and various others of them have separate ones.

The English have laboured (to their great expense) to find out the way by the seas to the north seas of Tartary to go into China, but by reason of the frozen seas, they have not yet prevailed. It has been reported that the Flemings have discovered that passage, which would very likely be to the great benefit of the northern parts of Christendom; yet that report is no longer made, and therefore it is to be thought that the Flemings have not proceeded so far.

---

[43] Timur (1336-1405) conquered large tracts of Asia and the Middle East, including India, Persia and Syria. He took prisoner Bayezid I, Sultan of the Ottoman Empire, at the Battle of Ankara in 1402, and held him captive until he died (possibly by dashing his brains out on the bars of his cage). Abbot may have known Christopher Marlowe's play Tamburlaine the Great, first performed in 1587.

Of Cathay, and China[44]

Next beyond Tartary, on the north-east part of Asia, lies a great country called Cathay, the bounds whereof extend themselves on the north and east, to the uttermost seas, and on the south to China. The people are not much learned, but more civil then the Tartars and have good and ordinary traffic with the countries adjoining.

This country has in it many kings, who are tributaries, and do owe obedience to one, whom they call the great Cham, or Khan, of Cathay, who is the chief governor of all the land, and esteemed for multitude of people and largeness of dominion, to be one of the great princes of the world. But his name is the less famous for that he lies so far distant from the best nations, and the passage into his country is so dangerous, either for the perils of the sea, or for the long space by land. His chief imperial city is called Cambalu[45].

On the south side of Cathay, and east part of Asia, next to the sea, lies China. This is a fruitful country, and yields as great store of rich commodities, as almost any country in the world. It contains in it very many several kingdoms, which are absolute princes in their seats.

The chief city in this country is called Quinsaie[46], and is described to be of incredible greatness, as were wont to be the ancient cities in the east, such as Babylon, Nineveh, and others.

This country was first discovered by the recent navigation of

---

[44] It was long thought that Cathay was a separate country, possibly with a partly Christian population. It was not until 1605 that Jesuits could confirm that China and Cathay were one and the same.

[45] The city named Cambalu by Marco Polo in his Travels (c. 1295) seems to have been Beijing.

[46] Hangzhou, a city described by Polo as "the finest and the noblest in the world".

the Portuguese into the East Indies[47].

The people of China are learned almost in all arts, very skilful workmen in curious fine works of all sorts, so that no country yields more precious merchandise than their workmanship. They are great soldiers, very politic and crafty, and in respect thereof condemning the wits of others, using a proverb, that all other nations see but with one eye, but they themselves with two.

It is reported that they have had from very ancient time among them these two things, which we hold to be the miracles of Christendom, and but lately invented. The one is the use of guns for the wars, and the other is printing, which they use not as we do, writing from the left hand to the right, or as the Hebrews and Syrians, from the right hand to the left, but directly downward, and so their lines at the top do begin again.

---

[47] The Portuguese landed in China in 1513.

Of the East Indies

On the south side of China, toward the Moluccan islands and the Indian Sea, lies the great country of India, extending itself from the south part of the Continent, by the space of many thousand miles westward, to the river Indus, which is the greatest river in all the country, except the Ganges, one of the greatest rivers in the world, which lies in the east part of the same Indies.

This is that country so famous in ancient time, for the great riches thereof, for the multitude of people, and for the conquest of Bacchus over it[48].

It is renowned also for the passage there of Alexander the Great[49,] throughout all the length of Asia and for his adventuring to go into the south Ocean with so mighty a fleet, which few or none had ever attempted before him.

Certainly there it was that Solomon did send once in three years for his gold and other rich merchandise: for the Scripture saith[50], that he sent his Fleet from Ezion-Geber, which stood upon the mouth of the Red Sea, and it was the directest passage which he had to the eastern Indies, whereas if his purpose had been to send to Peru, as some lately have imagined[51], his course would have been through the Mediterranean Sea, and the Straits of Gibraltar.

This country had in ancient times many absolute kingdoms and

---

[48] According to an epic poem by Nonnos (5th century AD).

[49] 327-325 BC; the 'south Ocean' was the Persian Gulf, to which Alexander sent an exploratory expedition.

[50] I Kings 9:26-29, which states that Solomon sent to Ophir for this treasure; Ezion-Geber was a biblical seaport on the northern extremity of the Gulf of Aqaba.

[51] Benito Arias Montano, Spanish scholar and churchman, suggested in 1571 that Ophir was located in Peru; other contemporary ideas include Great Zimbabwe and Mozambique, though current opinion – with Abbot - tends to identify it as being in either modern Pakistan or India.

provinces: in it were many philosophers, and men of great learning whom they called Gymnosophists[52], of whom was Calanus[53,] who burnt himself before Alexander.

The men of the south part of India are black. All sorts of creatures that are bred there are of incredible bigness, in respect of other countries, as their elephants, apes, monkeys, ants and others.

The riches hereof have been very great, with abundance of gold, insomuch that the area which is now called Malacca, was in times past named Aurea Chersonesus [the Golden Peninsula]. The quantities of spice that comes from there is exceeding great.

The Portuguese were the first who by their long navigations through the tropics and past the farthermost part of Africa have of late years[54] discovered these countries to Christendom. They fell into the hands of the King of Portugal, so now the King of Spain is reputed owner of them.

The Portuguese found several kingdoms at their first arrival in those parts, Calicut, Cambay, Cannanore, Cochin, and very many others. At first they joined with the kings for trade, but having been given leave to build castles for their defence, they have since by policy encroached into their hands a great part of the country, which covers the space of many thousand miles, altogether. The King of Spain has there a Viceroy, whose residence is commonly in the imperial city called Goa. Every year they send home great store of rich commodities into Spain.

The people of the country when the Portuguese came first there, were for the most part pagans, believing in no one god. Yes, to this day there are divers of them who do adore the sun as their god, and every morning at the rising thereof, do use very superstitious ceremonies, which our merchants who do trade to

---

[52] It was the Greeks, notably Plutarch in the 1st century AD, who gave them this name, which means 'naked philosophers' ; they were probably ascetics such as sadhus or yogis.

[53] Who, having caught pneumonia, set fire to himself so that he should be no burden on others.

[54] The expedition led by Vasco da Gama, in 1498.

Aleppo do often see; for divers of these Indians do come there with merchandise.

But the Saracens from the Gulfs of Persia and Arabia, who reverence the Prophet Mahomet, do traffic much there, so that Mahomet was known among them. But in one town, Cranganore [Kodungallur] they found certain Christians, dissenting in many things from the Church of Rome, and rather agreeing with the Protestants, which Christians had received their religion by succession, from the time of Thomas the Apostle; by whom (as it is recorded in the ancient ecclesiastical history[55]) part of India was converted.

In this country of India are many great and potent kings and kingdoms, which had been altogether unknown and unheard of in our part of the world, had we not been beholden to the Portuguese for their discovery. Before their navigation there from the other side of Africa we had only some stories from the Venetians, who traded and travelled there by land out of Turkey.

---

[55] As in the writings of St Ambrose of Milan in the 4th century.

Of Persia

There be divers countries between India and Persia; but they are not famous. Persia is a large country, which lies far west from India. It has on the north Assyria and Media, on the west Syria and the Holy Land, but next to it Mesopotamia. On the south is the main Ocean, which enters in notwithstanding by a bay called the Persian Gulf.

This is that country, which in ancient time was so renowned for its great riches and empire. These were they who took from the Assyrians the monarchy, and did set up in their country the second great empire, which began under Cyrus and continued to that Darius, who was overthrown by Alexander the Great. In this country reigned the great kings, Cyrus, Cambyses, Darius, the great Xerxes, Artaxerxes, and many other; which in profane writings are famous for their wars against the Scythians, Egyptians, and Greeks, and in the Scriptures, for the delivery of the Jews from Babylon by Cyrus, for the building of the second Temple at Jerusalem, and for many things which are mentioned of them in the Prophecy of Daniel.

The people of this nation were in former times very wild and uncontrolled, by reason of their great wealth, yet after they lost their monarchy by the Macedonians, they became great soldiers.

And therefore they did ever strongly defend themselves against the old Romans; so in the time of Constantine, and the other Emperors, they were feared neighbours to the Roman government. Of late time, they have strongly opposed themselves against the Turks, and have acquitted themselves well against them.

And yet notwithstanding in the days of Amurath III father to Mahomet the Turk now reigning [Mehmed III reigned 1595 – 1603], the Turk had the upper hand over the Persian, going so far with his army, as that he took the strong city Tauris standing within the Persian dominions, near to the Caspian Sea. But this loss was to be attributed partly to the great dissensions which were among the Persians themselves, and partly to the multitude of the Turkish soldiers, who with reinforcements overcame the Persians, although they slew many thousands of them.

They fight commonly on horseback and are governed as in time past by a king, so now by an absolute ruler, and a mighty Prince, whom they term the Shah, or Sophy[56] of Persia. He has many Countries, and small kings in Assyria, and Media, and the Countries adjoining, which are tributaries.

Among the Sophies of Persia, about 100 years since, there was one of great power, called Ismail [reigned 1502–24], who procured to himself great fame by his many and valorous attempts against the Turk. It is said that the Jews were strongly of opinion that he was that Messiah whom to this day they expect, and therefore hoped that he should have been their deliverer and advancer: but it fell out so clean contrary, that there was no man who more vexed and grieved them, than that Ismail did.

The Persians are all at this day Saracens in religion, believing in Mahomet: but as Papists and Protestants do differ in opinion concerning the same Christ, so do the Turks and Persians about their Mahomet, the one pursuing the other as heretics, with most deadly hatred, insomuch that there is, in this respect, almost continual wars between the Turk and the Persians[57].

---

[56] The Shah of Persia was long known in Western Europe as the Sophy (a title derived from the name of the Sufi dynasty).

[57] The former being predominantly Sunni and the latter Shiite.

Of Parthia and Media

On the north-east side of Persia, lies that country called Parthia, which in old time fought great wars against the Romans.

This country bounds on Media by the west, and it was in ancient time very full of people: whose fight as it was very much on horseback, so the manner of them continually was for to make an onset, and then to retreat, only to return again, like to the wild Irish[58]; so that no man was sure when he had obtained any victory over them.

These were the people that gave the great overthrow to that rich Marcus Crassus[59] of Rome, who by reason of his covetousness (intending more to his getting of gold, than to the guiding of his army) was slain himself, and many thousands of the Romans. The Parthians by way of reproach of his thirst after money, poured molten gold into his mouth after he was dead.

Against these, the great Lucullus[60] fought many battles; but the Romans were never able to bring them quite to subjection.

On the west side of Parthia, (having the Caspian Sea on the north, Armenia on the west, and Persia on the south) lies the country which in time past was called Media, but which is at this day governed by many inferior kings and princes, who are tributaries, and are subject to the Sophy of Persia. So that he is the Sovereign Lord of all Media, as our Englishmen have found who,

[58] For most of the 16th century there was prolonged guerrilla warfare in Ireland.

[59] Crassus (115 BC – 53 BC) Roman Consul and Triumvir, led the forces which suppressed the slave revolt of Spartacus; defeated and killed by the Parthians at the Battle of Carrhae. One of the richest men in ancient Rome. Cassius Dio tells the story of how the Parthians posthumously punished his greed.

[60] Lucius Licinius Lucullus (c. 118-57 BC) Roman Consul and an accomplished general; he invested much of his spoils from these wars on banqueting and the promotion of culture.

passing through the dominion of the Emperor of Russia, have crossed the Caspian Sea and traded with the inhabitants.

This nation in former times was very famous, for the Medes were they that took their empire from the Assyrians. When by Cyrus[61] it was joined to that of the Persians, it was very mighty, and was called by the name of the empire of the Medes and Persians. Here it was that Astyages, the grandfather of Cyrus, reigned [585-550 BC].

The chief city of this kingdom was called Ecbatana, as the chief city of Persia was Babylon.

It is to be observed of the kings of Media that in the summer time they did used to retire themselves northward to Ecbatana, for avoiding of the heat, but in the winter time they came down more south to Susa, which as it seemed was a warmer place. So they were both known as imperial cities, and chief residences of the kings of Media; which being known, takes away some of the confusion in old stories. The like custom was afterward used also by the kings of Persia.

---

[61] Cyrus the Great (559-530 BC) founded the Persian Empire; renowned not only for many military achievements but also for freeing the Jews from their Babylonian captivity and allowing them to return to Israel and rebuild the Temple.

Of Armenia and Assyria

On the western side of the Caspian Sea and of Media, lies a country called by a general name Armenia, which by some is distinctly divided into three parts. The north part whereof, being but little, is called Georgia; the middle part Turcomania[62]; the third part, by the proper name of Armenia. By which a man may see the reason of the differences between various writers, some saying that the country whence the Turks first came, was Armenia, some saying Turcomania, and some Georgia; the truth being, that out of one, or all these countries they did descend.

These Turks are supposed to be the issue of them whom Alexander the Great did shut up within certain mountains near to the Caspian Sea.

There is this one thing memorable in Armenia, that after the great Flood, the Ark of Noah did rest itself on the Mountains of Armenia, where, as Josephus[63] witnessed, it is to be seen yet to this day; the hills whereon it rests are called by some Noah's Mountains.

The people of this nation have retained amongst them the Christian Faith, as it is thought, from the time of the Apostle, but at this day it is spotted with many absurdities. Among other errors which the Church of Armenia has been noted to hold, this is one, that they did bathe their children, waving them up and down in flames of fire, and repute that to be a necessary circumstance of baptism. This error arises by mistaking that place of John the Baptist, where he said that he that came after him (meaning Christ)

---

[62]Turcomania, a region with very fluid boundaries, roughly corresponding perhaps with parts of Anatolia.

[63] Josephus (37-100 AD), Jewish historian, was by no means the last writer to mention the supposed continuing existence of the Ark.

should baptize them with the Holy Ghost, and with fire [Matthew 3.11]. In which place the word does not signify material fire, but expresses the lively and purging operation of the Spirit, like to the nature of fire.

On the south part of Armenia, bending towards the east, lies the country of Assyria, which is bounded on the west with Mesopotamia. This country was that land wherein the first monarchy was settled, which began under Ninus[64], whom the Scripture called Nimrod[65], living not long after Noah's Flood, and it ended in Sardanapulus[66], continuing 1300 years. The king of this country was Sennacherib, of whom we read in the Book of the Kings [2 Kings 19:35]; and here reigned Nebuchadnezzar, who took Jerusalem, and led the Jews away prisoners to Babylon.

In this country, is the swift river Tigris, near which was Paradise [the Garden of Eden]. Upon this river stood the great city Nineveh, which was almost of incredible bigness, and exceeding populous, by the nearness of the river, and marvellous fruitfulness of the soil, which, as Herodotus writes, did return their corn sometime 200, and sometimes 300 fold, and did yield sufficiency for to maintain it. This city for a long time was the imperial seat of the monarchy; but being destroyed (as God foretold it should be [Nahum 2], by the Chaldeans) the residence of the king was afterwards removed to Babylon, a great city in Chaldea, first built by Semiramis.

---

[64] Mythological founder of Nineveh.

[65] Genesis 10.8-9: "Nimrod … began to be a mighty one in the earth"; great-grandson of Noah.

[66] In classical literature, last king of Assyria.

Of Chaldea

Next to Assyria, lies Chaldea, having on the east side Assyria; on the west Syria or Palestine; on the north Armenia; on the south the desert of Arabia.

This country is often called by the name of Mesopotamia [Greek: *between the rivers*], which name it has, because it lies in the middle of two great rivers, Tigris and Euphrates. It is called also by the name of Babylonia; which word, of itself properly taken, does signify only that part of the country which stands about Babylon.

The chief city whereof was Babylon, whose ruins do remain to this day. It was a rich and most pleasant city for all kind of delight; and was in the latter time of that monarchy, the imperial city of the Assyrians, where Nebuchadnezzar and their other great kings did lie.

It was to this city that the children of Israel were carried as captives, which thereof was called the Captivity of Babylon. The kings of Persia also did keep their residence here. It was built upon the river Euphrates, some part of it standing on the one side, and some part on the other, having for its foundress Semiramis, the wife of Ninus.

Ammianus Marcellinus [4ᵗʰ century Roman historian] reports one thing of this country, wherein the admirable power of God does appear. He writes that in these parts are a huge number of lions, which were like enough to devour up both men and beasts throughout the country: but by reason of the store of water and mud thereof, there do breed yearly an innumerable company of gnats, whose property is to fly to the eye of the lion, as being a bright and orient [lustrous] thing; with this biting and stinging the lion tears so fiercely with his claws, that he puts out his own eyes, and by that means many are drowned in the rivers, others starve for want of prey, and many are the more easily killed by the inhabitants.

In this Mesopotamia, between the rivers Tigris and Euphrates, Paradise did stand. This was the country wherein Abraham the patriarch was born, and a country to which the Romans could very hardly extend their dominion, for they had much to do to get the government of anything beyond the river Euphrates. From this people it is thought the wise men came who brought presents to Christ, by the guiding of the Star.

For as in India, and all the eastern parts, so especially in this country, their noblemen, and priests, and very many people, do give themselves to all arts of divination. Here were the great soothsayers, enchanters, and wise men, as they call them. Here were the first astrologers, which are so described, and derided in the Scripture [e.g. Isaiah 47.13-14]. The Romans made laws against the astrologers of Babylon and Chaldea, who in Tully's *De Divinatione* [On Divination, by Cicero, 44 BC, Book I] and Tacitus [*Annals and Histories*, c100 AD], are ordinarily called by the name of Chaldeans, and indeed from these, and from the Egyptians, is supposed to have sprung the first knowledge of astronomy.

It is thought that a great reason whereof these Chaldeans were expert in the laudable knowledge of astronomy was partly because the country is so flat, that being without hills, they might more fully and easily discover the whole face of the Heaven. Partly, because the old fathers who lived so long, not only before, but in some good part also after the flood of Noah, did dwell in, or near to these parts, and they by observation of their own did find out and discover many things of the heavenly bodies, which they delivered as from hand to hand in their posterity.

But as corruption does stain the best things, so in process of time, the true astronomy was defiled with superstitious rules of astrology (which caused the Prophets Isaiah and Jeremiah so bitterly to inveigh against them). And then, in their fabled stories they would report that they had in their records observations for 25,000 years, which must need be a very great untruth, unless we will qualify it as some have done, taking their years, not by the revolution of the Sun, but of the Moon, whose course is ended in the space of a month.

Of Asia Minor

On the north-west side of Mesopotamia lies that country which is now called Anatolia but in times past Asia Minor, having on the north side the Black Sea, on the west the Hellespont, and on the south, the main Mediterranean. In the ancient writings both of the Greeks and of the Romans, this is often called by the single name of Asia, because it was best known to them, and they were not so much acquainted with the farther places of Asia the great.

This country in general, for the fruitfulness of the land, standing in so temperate a climate, and for the convenience of the sea every way, and so many good harbours, has been reputed always a very commodious and pleasureful country. It is wholly at this day under the Turk. The Taurus Mountains go along from the west to the east part of it.

The greatness of this country is such, that it has comprehended many kingdoms and large provinces, besides cities of great fame. On the south east part thereof, near to Palestine, lies Cilicia, the chief city whereof is Tarsus, the country of Saint Paul; the place where Solomon sent for great store of his gold, and provision for the Temple, where Jonah also fled, when he should have gone to Nineveh.

In the straits of this Cilicia, near to the Taurus Mountains, did Alexander give a great overthrow in person to Darius, in the joining of their first battle [Battle of Issus, 333 BC].

This place seems to have been very fortunate for great fights; in as much as there also near to the straits, was the battle fought out between Severus the Emperor and Niger [Pescennius Niger, defeated at Issus AD 194], Governor of Syria, who aspired to the Empire, but in a battle which was very hardly fought out, he was overthrown in the straits of Cilicia.

In the very corner where Cilicia is joined to the upper part of

Syria, is a little bay, which in times past was named *Sinus Isicus*, near to which Alexander built one of his cities, which he called by his own name. But howsoever in times past it was named Alexandria, it is now by the Venetians and other Christians called Alexandretta; as who should say, little Alexandria, in comparison of the other. In Egypt the Turks do call it Scandarond, and it is a small harbour, where our merchants do land most of their goods, which are afterwards by Camels carried up to Aleppo. At this day the city is so decayed, that there be only a few houses there.

Westward from Cilicia lies the provinces called Pamphylia, wherein stands the city of Seleucia, built by Seleucus[67], one of the four great successors of Alexander the Great.

On the west of this Pamphylia, stands Lycia, and more west from thence, near the isle of Rhodes, is Caria, one of the sea towns whereof is Halicarnassus, which was the country of Herodotus [5th century BC], which is one of the most ancient historians that is extant of the Gentiles, and who dedicated his nine books to the honour of the Muses.

Here also was that Dionysus born, who is called commonly Dionysus Halicarnassus [c60-7 BC], one of the writers of Roman history, for the first 300 years after Rome was built.

The whole country of Caria is sometimes signified by the name of this Halicarnassus, although it was but one city; and thereupon Artemisia, who in the days of Xerxes came to aid him against the Grecians, and behaved herself so manfully in a great fight at sea [Salamis, 480 BC], where Xerxes stood by as a coward, is entitled by the name not of Queen of Caria, but of Halicarnassus.

Also in the days of Alexander the great, there was another Queen, named Ada[68], who is also honoured by the title of Queen of Halicarnassus.

---

[67] In fact the city founded by Seleucus (358–281 BC) seems to have been on the west bank of the Tigris, not in Pamphylia.

[68] Sister of Mausolus (377–353 BC) whose grand tomb gave us the word mausoleum

We have thus far described those cities of which do lie from Syria, along the sea coast westward, but these are but the southern part of Asia Minor.

Now upwards towards the north, stands Ionia, where those did dwell, who were likely to have joined with Xerxes in the great battle at sea but that Themistocles [524–459 BC, Athenian statesman] by a policy did win them from him, to take part with the Greeks.

Diodorus Siculus [1st century BC, Greek historian] writes, that the Athenians, who professed to be kin to those Ionians, were once marvellously persistent importunate with them, that they should leave their own country, and come and dwell with them. The Ionians at length did accept, but the Athenians had no place to put them in, and so they returned, with great disgrace to them both.

A little within the land, lying north and east from Ionia, was Lydia which some time was the kingdom of Croesus, who was reputed so rich a king, When he was in his prosperity, proclaiming his happiness, he was told by Solon that no man could reckon upon happiness while he still lived, because there might be great mutability of Fortune, which he afterward found true. For he was taken prisoner by Cyrus, who was once minded to have put him to death; but hearing him report the words of Solon formerly given to him, he was moved to think that it might be his own case, and so took pity on him, and spared his life.

These Lydians being forbidden afterward by Cyrus to use any armour, did give themselves to baths and stews[69] , and other such effeminate things.

Upon the sea coast in Ionia, stands the city Ephesus, which was one of the seven cities, to which John in his Revelations did write his seven Epistles, and St Paul also directed his Epistle to the Ephesians, to the Church which was in this place.

This was one of the most renowned cities of Asia Minor. Its

---

[69] Stews: sometimes meaning brothels, but originally a room with hot air or steam – a sort of sauna.

fame did most arise from the Temple of Diana, which was there built, and was reputed for the magnificence thereof as one of the Seven Wonders of the World. This Temple was said to be 200 years in building, and was burnt several times, for the most part by lightning, and the final destruction thereof came by a base person, called Herostratus, who to purchase himself some fame, did set it on fire[70].

This was the place where it is said in the Acts of the Apostles [Acts 19:27], that all Asia, and the whole world, did worship this Diana.

Cicero reported in his De Natura Deorum, that the reason why the Temple of Diana was set on fire the same night when Alexander the Great was borne, was given in jest that the Mistress of it was from home; because she being the Goddess of Midwives, did that night wait upon Olympias the mother of Alexander the Great, who was brought to bed in Macedonia.

Another of the seven cities to which John did write is Smyrna, standing also in Ionia upon the sea coast, but somewhat more north than Ephesus.

This is the place there Polycarp was Bishop [in the 2nd century AD], who had once been a disciple of John the Evangelist, and, living till he was of great age, was at last put to death for Christ's sake. The Governor of the country had urged him to deny his Saviour, and to burn incense to an idol. But he answered, that fourscore and six years he had served Christ Jesus, and in all that time he had never done him harm; and therefore now in his old age he would not begin to deny him.

The third city to which the Epistle is directed in the Apocalypse is Sardis, which stands within the land in Lydia, as is described by the best writers. It was a city both of great pleasure and profit to the kings in whose dominion it stood. This may be gathered because when once the Greeks had won it, Darius or Xerxes, who

---

[70] To deter imitation, the city executed Herostratus and forbade on pain of death any mention of his name.

were kings of Persia, did give charge, that every day at dinner, he should be reminded that the Greeks had taken Sardis; which intended, that he never was in quiet, till it might be recovered again.

There stood also inland, Philadelphia, Thyateira, Laodicea, and most of all to the north, Pergamon, which were the other four cities unto which Saint John the Evangelist did direct his Epistle.

Going upward from Ionia to the north, there lies on the sea coast a little country, called Aeolis: and beyond that, although not upon the sea, the two provinces called Asia Major, and Mysia, which in times past, was so base and contemptible, that the people thereof were used in speech as a Proverb, so that if a man wanted to describe someone as meaner than the meanest, it was said, he was *Mysiorum postremus* [worse than the Mysians].

On the west part of Mysia did lie the country called Troas, wherein stood Ilium, and the city of Troy, against which, as both Virgil and Homer have written, the Greeks did continue their siege for the space of ten years, by reason that Paris had stolen away Helen, the wife of Menelaus, who was king of Sparta.

Eastward both from Troas and Mysia, a good space within the land, was the country called Phrygia, where the Goddess which was called *Bona Dea*[71] had her first abiding, and from there was brought to Rome, so that good fortune should follow her thither.

In this country lived that Gordius, who knit the knot, called for the intricateness thereof, *Nodus Gordianus*[72] [the Gordian Knot]. When it could not be untied, it was cut in sunder by Alexander the Great, supposing that it should be his fortune, for the loosing of it so, to be the conqueror, and king of Asia, as by a prophecy of the same Gordius had been before spoken.

Yet northward from Phrygia lies the country of Bithynia, which

---

[71] "The good goddess" was worshipped especially by women, who were forbidden to reveal her true name, Fauna, to men.

[72] The Gordian Knot, a complex knot which was regarded as impossible to undo; Alexander cut it through with his sword.

was once a kingdom where Prusias reigned[73], that had so much to do with the Romans.

In this country stands the city Nicaea, where the first General Council [of the Church, in AD 325] was called by Constantine the Great against Arius the Heretic. Here stands also Chalcedon, where the fourth General Council [in AD 451] was held by the Emperor Marcian, against the heretic Nestorius.

From Bithynia eastward, on the north side of Asia Minor, stands the country of Paphlagonia, where was the city built by Pompey the Great, called by his name, Pompeiopolis[74].

On the south of Paphlagonia did stand the country of Galatia, whereunto Saint Paul wrote his Epistle to the Galatians. This also was one of those countries where the Jews were dispersed, unto whom Saint Peter wrote his first Epistle, as also unto them which were in Pontus, Cappadocia, and Bithynia.

Southward lies the province termed Lycaonia, and from there yet more south, bordering upon Pamphylia, which touches the Mediterranean Sea, lies Pisidia; concerning which countries we find often times mention made in stories which touch upon Asia Minor.

From these southern parts, if we return back again unto the north and east of Asia Major, lies the kingdom of Pontus, neighbouring the Black Sea.

In this Pontus did reign [119-63 BC] Mithridates, who in younger days had travelled over the greatest part of Asia, and is reported to have been so skilful, that he could well speak more than 20 languages. His hatred was ever great towards the Romans, against whom he so combined with the natives of those parts, that in one night they slew more than 70,000 of the Romans, carrying their intention so secret that it was revealed by none, until the

---

[73] Prusius, (c. 228-182 BC) gave shelter to Hannibal after Rome had defeated Carthage in the Punic Wars.

[74] Now Taşköprü, in the Black Sea region of Turkey – apparently a town noted for its garlic.

execution was done[75].

Pompey the Great was the man who distressed this Mithridates, and brought him to such an extremity, that he would gladly have poisoned himself, but could not, as his stomach had become so used to that kind of treacle[76] (which by reason of his inventing of, to this day is called Mithridate) made of a kind of poison, so that no venom would easily work upon him[77].

Southward from this Pontus stands the old kingdom of Cappadocia, which in times past was observed to have many men in it, but little money. Whence Horace saith: *mancipii locuples eget aris Cappadocum Rex*[78].

Eastward from this Cappadocia, as also from Pontus, is Armenia Minor; whereof the things memorable, are described in the other Armenia. And thus much touching Asia Minor.

---

[75] An incident known as the Asiatic Vespers, in 88 BC.

[76] From theriac, a compound of 60-70 ingredients, including a viper, mixed with honey, supposed to be an antidote against all poisons; a Venetian speciality.

[77] As AE Housman puts it in *A Shropshire Lad*:

There was a king reigned in the East/ There, when kings will sit to feast,

They get their fill before they think/ With poisoned meat and poisoned drink.

He gathered all the springs to birth/ From the many-venomed earth;

First a little, thence to more, / He sampled all her killing store;

And easy, smiling, seasoned sound, / Sate the king when healths went round.

They put arsenic in his meat /And stared aghast to watch him eat;

They poured strychnine in his cup /And shook to see him drink it up:

They shook, they stared as white's their shirt: / Them it was their poison hurt.

I tell the tale that I heard told. / Mithridates, he died old.

[78] "The king of Cappadocia, rich in slaves [but] short of cash", Satires I.6, 39, Quintus Horatius Flaccus, 65-8 BC.

Of Syria and Palestine, or the Holy land

Outward from Cilicia and Asia Minor lies Syria, a part whereof was called Palestine, having on the east Mesopotamia, on the south Arabia, on the west Tyre and Sidon, and at the end of the Mediterranean Sea.

The people of Syria were in times past called the Aramaeans, in whose language is the Syriac [Aramaic] translation of the New Testament.

In this country stands Antioch, which was sometime one of the ancient Patriarchates, and is a city of reckoning to this day. Here also stands now the city of Aleppo, which is a famous market town for the merchandising of the Persians, and others of the east, and for the Turks, and such countries as be adjoining. Here stands also Tripoli.

The south part of Syria lying down towards Egypt and Arabia, was the place where the children of Israel did dwell, being a country of small quantity, not 200 Italian miles[79] in length: it was so fruitful flowing with milk and honey (as the Scripture called it) that it did maintain above 30 kings and their people, before the coming of the children of Israel out of Egypt, and was sufficient afterwards to support the incredible number of the twelve tribes of Israel.

It is noted of this country that whereas by the goodness of the climate wherein it stood, and the fertility of the soil, (but especially by the blessing of God) it was the most fruitful land that was in the World.

Now our travellers by experience do find the country, in

---

[79] "The Romans of old held 1000 paces for a mile, and such are the miles of Italy. A common English mile makes one and a half Italian long." Fynes Moryson, An Itinerary, 1617.

respect of the fruitfulness, to be changed, God cursing the land together with the Jews, the inhabitants of it. It is observed also for all the eastern parts, that they are not so fertile as they have been in former ages, the Earth (as it were) growing old, which is an argument of the dissolution to come by the Day of Judgement.

Through this country does run the river Jordan, which has been famous for the fruitfulness of the trees standing thereupon, and for the mildness of the air, so that (as Josephus writes) when snow has been in other places of the land, about the river it has been so calm, that men did go in single thin linen garments.

In this country stands the Asphalt Lake, so called because of a kind of slime called bitumen, or asphalt, which daily it does cast up, having the force to join stones exceeding fast in building; and into this Lake does the river Jordan run.

This Lake is called the Dead Sea, a sea, because it is salt; and dead, for that no living thing is therein. The water thereof is so thick that few things will sink therein, insomuch that Josephus saith, that an ox having all his legs bound, will not sink into that water.

The Lake (as it was supposed) was turned into this quality, when God did destroy Sodom and Gomorrah, and the cities adjoining, with fire and brimstone from heaven: for Sodom and the other cities did stand near to the Jordan, and to this Dead Sea. The destruction of which all that coast to this day is a witness, the earth smelling of brimstone, being desolate, and yielding no fruit saving apples, which grow with a fair show to the eye, like other fruit, but as soon as they are touched, do turn presently to soot or ashes.

The land of Palestine had for its inhabitants, all the twelve tribes of Israel, which were under one kingdom, until the time of Rehoboam the son of Solomon; but then were they divided into two kingdoms, ten tribes being called Israel, and two Judah, whose chief city was called Jerusalem [2 Chronicles 10].

The ten tribes, after much idolatry, were carried prisoners to Assyria, and the kingdom dissolved, other peoples taking their place in Samaria and the country adjoining.

The other two tribes were properly called the Jews, and their land, Judea, which continued long after in Jerusalem and thereabouts, until the Captivity of Babylon, where they lived for seventy years. They were afterward restored, but lived without glory, until the coming of Christ. But since this time for a curse upon them and their children they are scattered upon the face of the Earth, as runagates, without certain country, king, priest, or prophet.

In their chief city, Jerusalem, was the Temple of God, first most gloriously built by Solomon and afterward destroyed by Nebuchadnezzar. By the commandment of Cyrus king of Persia, was a second Temple built, much more base than the former. For besides the poverty, and smallness of it, there wanted five things which were in the former, as the Jews write: first, the Ark of the Covenant: secondly, the pot of Manna: thirdly, the Rod of Aaron: fourthly, the two Tables of the Law, written by the finger of God: and fifthly, the fire of the Sacrifice, which came down from heaven.

Herod the Great, an Edomite stranger, having got the kingdom, contrary to the Law of Moses, and knowing the people to be offended therewith, to procure their favour did build a third Temple, wherein our Saviour Jesus Christ and his Apostles did teach.

The city of Jerusalem was twice taken, and utterly laid desolate, first, by Nebuchadnezzar, at the captivity of Babylon and secondly, after the death of Christ, by Vespasian the Roman, (who first began the Wars) and by his son Titus, who was afterward Emperor of Rome, who brought such horrible desolation on that city, and the people thereof, by fire, sword, and famine, that the like has not been read in any history. He did afterwards put thousands of them (on some one day) to be devoured of the beasts, which was a cruel custom of the Roman magnificence.

Although numbers and times be not superstitiously to be observed (as many foolish imagine) yet it is a matter in this place, not unworthy the noting, which Josephus reports, that the very same day whereon the Temple was set on fire by the Babylonians, was the day whereon the second Temple was set on fire by the Romans, and that was upon the tenth day of August.

After this destruction, the land of Judea, and the ruins of Jerusalem, were possessed by some of the people adjoining, until after about 600 years the Saracens did invade it, for expelling of whom from thence, divers Frenchmen and other Christians, under the leading of Godfrey of Bouillon, did assemble themselves, thinking it a great shame, that the holy land, (as they called it) the city of Jerusalem, and the place of the sepulchre of Christ, should be in the hands of infidels[80].

This Godfrey ruled in Jerusalem with the title of Duke: but his successors after him, for the space of 87 years, called themselves Kings of Jerusalem. About which time, Saladin (who called himself King of Egypt and Asia Minor) did win it from the Christians. For the recovery whereof, Richard I, King of England, together with the French king, and the King of Sicily, did go in person with the armies to Jerusalem; but although they won many things from the infidels, yet the end was, that the Saracens did retain the Holy Land.

Roger Hovedon [12th century English historian] in his life of Henry II of England, does give this memorable note, that at the time when the cities of Jerusalem and Antioch were taken out of the hand of the pagans by the means of Godfrey of Bouillon and others of his company, the Pope of Rome that then was, was called Urbanus, the Patriarch of Jerusalem, Heraclius and the Holy Roman Emperor, Frederick; and at the same time when the said Jerusalem was recovered again by Saladin, the Pope's name was Urbanus, that of the Patriarch of Jerusalem, Heraclius, and of the Holy Roman Emperor, Frederick.

The whole country and city of Jerusalem are now in the dominion of the Turk, who for a great toll does suffer many

---

[80] Godfrey was a leader of the First Crusade (1096-1099) and after the capture of Jerusalem in 1099 became the first ruler of the Kingdom of Jerusalem until his death in the next year.

Christians to abide there.

There are now therefore two or more monasteries, and religious houses, where Friars do abide, and make a good commodity of showing the Sepulchre of Christ and other monuments to such Christian pilgrims as do superstitiously to go on pilgrimage to the Holy Land.

The King of Spain was wont to call himself King of Jerusalem.

Of Arabia

Next to the Holy Land lies the great country of Arabia, having on the north part Palestine and Mesopotamia, on the east side, the Gulf of Persia, on the south, the main ocean of India or Ethiopia, on the west Egypt and the great bay, called the Red Sea.

This country is divided into three parts. The north part is called *Arabia Deserta* [Desert Arabia], the south part, which is the greatest, is named *Arabia Felix* [Happy Arabia], and the middle between both that (which for the abundance of rocks and stones) is called *Arabia Petrea* [Rocky Arabia].

The desert of Arabia, is that place in the which God after the deliverance of the Israelites from Egypt by passing through the Red Sea, did keep his people under Moses, for 40 years, because of their rebellion, feeding them in the meantime with manna from heaven and sometimes with water miraculously drawn out of dry rocks. For the country has very little water, almost no trees, and is utterly unfit for tillage or corn. There are no towns nor inhabitants of this desert: in *Arabia Petrea* are some, but not many.

Arabia Felix for fruitfulness of ground, and convenient standing every way towards the sea, is one of the best countries of the world. The principal cause why it is called happy is because it yields many things in abundance, which in other parts of the world are to be had, such as frankincense, especially, the most precious balms, myrrh, and many other both fruits and spices, and it also yields some precious stones.

When Alexander the Great was young, after the manner of the Macedonians, he was to put incense upon an altar, and pouring on great store of frankincense, one of the nobility of his country told him, that he was too prodigal of that sweet perfume, and that he should make spare, until he had conquered the land wherein the frankincense did grow. But when afterwards Alexander had taken possession of Arabia, he sent a ship load of frankincense to the nobleman, and bade him serve the gods plentifully, and not offer incense miserably.

This is that country wherein Mahomet was born, who was brought up in his youth in the trade of merchandise. The book of his religion is called the Al-Koran. His followers, although they came of Hagar, the handmaid of Sarah, Abraham's wife, and therefore should of her be called Ishmaelites, term themselves Saracens, as coming from Sarah, because they would not seem to come of a bond-woman; they are called by some writers, Arabians, instead of Saracens, their name being drawn from their first country.

In this country of Arabia, stands a city called Mecca, where is the place where Mahomet was buried, and in remembrance of him there is built a great temple, unto which the Turks and Saracens do yearly go on pilgrimage, (as some Christians do to the Holy land). For they account Mahomet to be the greatest Prophet that ever came into the world: saying, that there were three great Prophets, Moses, Christ and Mahomet: and as the doctrine of Moses was bettered by Christ, so the doctrine of Christ is amended by Mahomet. In this respect, as we reckon the computation of our years from the incarnation of Christ, so the Saracens account theirs from the time of Mahomet.

The Turks [the Ottoman Empire] whose fame began now about 300 years since, have embraced the opinions and religion of the Saracens concerning Mahomet. Some of our Christians do report, that Medina a city, standing three days journey from Mecca, is the place where Mahomet was buried, and that by his own order his body was put into an iron coffin, which being carried into a temple, the roof or vault whereof was made of adamant, or perhaps of the loadstone, is attracted to the top of the vault, and there hangs, being supported by nothing. But there is no certainty of this narration[81].

---

[81] Apparently this European legend is unknown to Islamic writers.

On the west side of Arabia, between that and Egypt, lies the gulf called the Red Sea because the land and banks thereabout are (in colour) red. This is that sea, through the which the people of Israel were led by Moses, when they fled out of Egypt from Pharaoh, God causing by his power, the waters to stand on both sides of them, that they passed through as on dry land.

This is that sea, through which the spices of the East Indies were in times past brought to Alexandria in Egypt, and from there dispersed into Christendom by the Venetians. These spices and apothecaries' drugs are found to be far worse than before they were, by reason of the great moisture which they take from the water, by reason of the long navigation of the Portuguese by the back part of Africa.

This is that sea through which Solomon did send for his gold, and other precious merchandise to the East Indies, and not the West Indies, as some lately have disputed; that opinion would make it appear that America and the West Indies were known in the time of Solomon. But if he had sent thither, his course would have been along the Mediterranean, and through the straits of Gibraltar, between Spain and the Barbary Coast: but the Scripture tells that the fleet which Solomon sent forth was built at Ezion-Geber, which is said to stand on the Red Sea. So his course might be eastward, or southward, but not westward.

In the desert of Arabia is the Mount Horeb, which by some is supposed to be the same that is called the Mount Sinai, where many think it was that Abraham would have offered up his son Isaac. But this is certain, that it was the place where God in the wilderness did give to the people of Israel his Law of the Ten Commandments, in thundering, lightning, and great earthquake, in most fearful manner.

Of Africa and Egypt

From Arabia and Palestine, toward the west lies Africa, having on the north side, from one end of it to the other, the Mediterranean Sea. The greatest part of which country, although it has been guessed at by writers in former time, yet because of the great heat of it, lying for the most part of it in the tropical zone, and for the wilderness therein, it was in former time supposed by many, not to be much inhabited. It was very little discovered until the Portuguese began their navigation on the backside of Africa, to the East Indies. So exact a description is therefore not to be looked for, as has been of Asia and Europe.

Joining to the Holy land, by a little isthmus is the country of Egypt, which is a land as fruitful as any almost in the world, although in these days it does not answer to the fertility of former times.

This is that which in the time of Joseph did relieve Canaan with corn, and the family of Jacob which did so multiply in the land of Egypt, that they were grown to a huge multitude, when GOD by Moses did deliver them from there.

This country did yield exceeding abundance of corn to the city of Rome, whereupon Egypt, as well as Sicily, was commonly called the granary of the Roman people.

It is observed from all antiquity that almost never any rain did fall in the land of Egypt, so the raining with thunder and lightning, and fire running on the ground, was much more strange when God plagued Pharaoh, in the days of Moses. But the flooding of the river Nile over all the country (their cities only, and some few hills, excepted) does so water the Earth, that it brings forth fruit abundantly.

The flooding of this river yearly, is one of the greatest miracles of the world, no man being able to yield a sufficient and assured reason thereof, though many possible causes and opinions are put forward.

Heathen testimonies, and experience of travellers suggest that no rain falls in Egypt; it may be gathered also out of the Scripture, for in the 11th Chapter of Deuteronomy [11.10-1], God does make an antithesis between the lands of Canaan and Egypt, saying that Egypt was watered as a man would water a garden of herbs, that is to say, by hand: but they should come into a land which had hills, and mountains, and which was watered with the rain of heaven. Yet some have written, that every now and then there are mists in Egypt which yield, though not rain, yet a pretty dew.

It is noted of this river, that if it is under the height of 15 cubits, then for want of moisture, the earth is not fruitful, and if it above 17 cubits, that there is likely to be a dearth, by reason of the abundance of moisture, the water lying longer on the land than the inhabitants do desire.

It is conjectured that it is the falling and melting of snow in the Mountains of the Moon[82] which make the i6ncrease of the River Nile. The custom of the people in the southern parts of Arabia is that they receive into ponds and dams the water that so hastily falls, and the same they let out with sluices, one after another, which causes it to come down orderly into the plains of Egypt.

For the keeping up of these dams, the country of Egypt has time out of mind paid a great toll to Prester John[83]: when of late it was denied by the Turk, Prester John caused all the sluices to be let go on a sudden, whereby he marvellously annoyed, and drowned up a great part of the country of Egypt.

In Egypt learning has been very ancient, but especially the knowledge of astronomy and mathematics. Before the time of

---

[82] Believed in classical times to be situated in central Africa, and to be the source of the White Nile; their location and indeed existence is doubtful.

[83] In European fable, a mighty Christian priest-king whose realm was originally believed to be set in Asia, but by Abbot's time was held to be in Ethiopia; Prester comes from the Latin Presbyter, or priest. See *Of Abyssinia, and the Empire of Prester John, below.*

Cicero, their priests would report that they had the descent of 1500 years exactly recorded, with observations astrological. This is a fable, unless they reckon their years by the Moon (as some suppose they did, every month for a year) but it does argue knowledge to have been among them from very ancient times.

Their priests had among them a kind of writing, and describing of things by picture which they did call their hieroglyphics.

This in times past was a kingdom, and by the kings thereof were built those great Pyramids which were held to be one of the Seven Wonders of the World, being mighty huge buildings, erected of exceeding height, for to show the magnificence of their founders. There is part of two or three of them remaining to this day.

Several learned men are at this day of opinion that when the Children of Israel were in Egypt, and so oppressed by Pharaoh, as is mentioned in the beginning of the book of Exodus [1.11-14], that their labour in burning of brick was partly employed to the erecting of some of those Pyramids; but the Scripture does only mention walling of cities.

The Founders of these Pyramids were commonly buried, in, or under them: and it is not unfit to remember, that the kings and great men of Egypt, had much cost bestowed upon them after they were dead.

As Arabia was near to them, where they had most precious balms, and other costly spices, they did with charge embalm their dead, and that with such curious art, that the flesh thereof and the skin, would remain unputrefied for hundreds or thousands of years. Whereof experiments are plentiful at this day, by the whole bodies, hands, or other parts, the colour being very black, and the flesh clung to the bones, which by merchants are now brought from there. These make the mummia[84], which the apothecaries use.

---

[84] Resin or powder extracted from mummies, and used medicinally (according to Rupert Brooke in his poem, MUMMIA as an aphrodisiac) or in the practice of magic. (see footnote following page)

Moses speaks of this, when he says [Genesis, 50.2] that Jacob was embalmed by the physicians, after the manner of embalming of the Egyptians. But this manner of embalming is ceased long since in Egypt.

In Egypt did stand the great city Memphis, which at this day is called Cairo, one of the famous cities of the east.

Here did Alexander build that city which to this day is after his name called Alexandria, being now the greatest city of merchandise in all Egypt. Of which Ammianus Marcellinus [4th century Roman historian] observes, that there was never, or almost never, a day when the sun did not shine at least once over Alexandria. This city was one of the four Patriarchal Sees which were appointed in the first Nicene Council.

This country was governed by a king, as long ago as almost any country in the world. Here reigned Amasis [570-526 BC], who made those good laws spoken of by Herodotus and Diodorus Siculus [Greek historians], in whose writing, the ancient customs of the Egyptians are worthy to be read.

After Alexander's time, Ptolemy, one of his captains, took his kingdom, of whom all this successors were called Ptolemies, as beforehand all their kings were called Pharaohs. They continued long friends and in league with the people of Rome, until the time of Julius Caesar; but afterward they were subject to the Romans, until that empire did decay.

When they had withdrawn themselves from the Roman government, they set up a prince of their own, who they termed the Sultan of Egypt, of whom about 400 years ago Saladin was one. But when this race ran out, the Mamelukes (who were the guard of

---

MUMMIA

As those of old drank mummia/To fire their limbs of lead,

Making dead kings from Africa/Stand pandar to their bed;

Drunk on the dead, and medicined/With spiced imperial dust,

In a short night they reeled to find/Ten centuries of lust.

the Sultan, as the janissaries are to the Turk) appointed a prince at their pleasure. Until about a 100 years ago, or less [in fact, 1517], the Turk Selim possessed himself of the sole government of the country, so that at this day Egypt is wholly under the Turk.

There are Christians that now live in Egypt, paying their tribute to the Turk, as others do now also in Greece.

Aeneas Silvius [Pope Pius II] states that attempts were made to dig through that little isthmus or strait which at the top of the Red Sea joins Egypt to Arabia, or to the Holy Land, imagining the labour not to be great, for they conceived the space of ground to be no more than 1500 furlongs.

Sesostris [1878-1839 BC] the King of Egypt (as he says) did first attempt this. Secondly Darius, the great Monarch of the Persians. Thirdly Ptolemy [ruled 285-246 BC] one of the kings of Egypt, who drew a ditch 100 feet broad, 30 feet deep and 37½ miles long. But when he intended to go forward, he was forced to cease, for fear of inundation, and overflowing the whole land of Egypt, the Red Sea being found to be higher (by three cubits) then the ordinary plain of Egypt was. But Pliny affirmed that the digging was given over lest the sea being let in should mar the water of the Nile, which alone does yield drink to the Egyptians.

It is said that there was a Portuguese also, that of late years, had a conceit to have had this work finished, that so he might have made the third part of the old known world, Africa, to have been an island compassed round with the sea.

Men commonly in the description of Egypt do report that whole country to stand in Africa; but if we will speak exactly, and repute the Nile to be the boundary between Asia and Africa, we must then acknowledge that the eastern part of Egypt, from the Nile and so forward to the Red Sea, does lie in Asia.

Although this country of Egypt does stand in the self same climate that Mauritania does, yet the inhabitants there are not black, but rather dun, or tawny. Of which colour Cleopatra was observed to be, who by enticement so won the love of Julius Caesar and Antony. And of that colour do those runagates by devices make themselves to be, who go up and down the world under the name of Egyptians[85], being indeed but counterfeits and the refuse or rascality of many nations.

---

[85] Gypsies (Roma) who were thought at Abbot's time to have come from Egypt – rather than the Indian sub-continent, as is now believed.

Of Cyrene and Africa the Less

On the west side of Egypt lying along the Mediterranean, is a country which was called in old time Cyrene[86]; wherein [at the oasis of Siwa] did stand that oracle which was so famous in the time of Alexander the Great, called by the name of the temple or oracle of Jupiter Ammon, where when Alexander did repair, as to take council of himself, and his success, the Priests being before taught what they should say, did flatteringly profess him to be the Son of God, and that he was to be adored. So that as the oracle of Delphi, and some others, were plain delusions of Satan, who did reign in that dark time of ignorance, so this of Jupiter Ammon, may be well supposed to be nothing else, but a cousonage [fraudulent deceit] of the Priests.

In this country, and all near about where the oracle stood, are very great wildernesses, where did appear to Alexander for four days' journey, neither grass, tree, water, man, bird, nor beast, but only a deep kind of sand. So that he was enforced to carry water (and all other provision) with him for himself and his company on camels' backs.

At this day, this country has lost its old name, and is reckoned as a part of Egypt, and lies under the Turk.

In dry countries, as in Africa, and the wilderness of Arabia, they have much use of camels. First, because they can carry a huge burden of water and other provision. Secondly, because that themselves will go a long time without drink, travelling four days together without it, but then drinking excessively, and that especially of muddy and puddle water. And thirdly, because that, in an extremity, those that travel with them do let their blood, and suck it out; whereby although the owner is much relieved, the

---

[86] A Greek colony in what is now Libya.

camel is little the worse.

Westward from this country, along the Mediterranean, lies that part of Africa which was termed by the Romans, sometimes simply Africa, sometimes Africa the Less. In this country did stand that place so famous, mentioned by Sallust, under the name of Philenorum Arae, which was the boundary in that time, between Africa and Cyrene[87].

On the north and east part hereto, in the sea near to the shore, was that quicksand, which in times past did destroy so many ships, and was called Syrtis Magna: as also on the north and west part, was the other sand, called Syrtis of Egypt, whose dominion did extend itself so far to the west, and there was divided from the kingdom of Tunis, but it is now wholly under the Turk, and is commonly reputed as a part of Barbary.

For now, by a general name, from the confines of Cyrene to the west, as far as Hercules' pillar, is called Barbary; though it contain in it divers kingdoms, as Tunis, Fez and Morocco.

[87] It was famous from the 4th century BC legend of the Carthaginian Fileni brothers, who were buried alive by the Cyrenians to mark that boundary; much later it was the site of Mussolini's towering desert folly, known to the Eighth Army as "Marble Arch".

Of Mauritania Caesariensis

A part of that country which is called at this day Barbary has in old time been called Mauritania, which was divided into two parts: the east part whereof next to Africa the Less, was called by the Romans, Mauritania Caesariensis, as the other was called Mauritania Tingitana. In the former was the country of Numidia, the people whereof were used in the wars of the Carthaginians, as light horsemen; and for all nimble services were very active.

In the east part of the country standing next the sea, was that famous city of Carthage, supposed to be built by Dido, who came from Tyre.

This city was it, which for the space of some 100 years contended with Rome for the empire of the world. In the Roman histories are recorded the great wars which the people of Rome had with the city of Carthage.

In the first war of the three, the contention was for the isles of Sicily, Corsica, and Sardinia. The victory fell to the Romans, and the Carthaginians were glad to redeem their peace with the leaving of the islands.

The second war was begun by Hannibal, who broke the league, and after he had taken some part of Spain from the Romans, and sacked Sagunto [Spain], a city of their friends, came first over the Pyrenee hills to France then over the Alps to Italy. Here he overthrew the Romans in three great battles, and much endangered their estate. He continued in Italy with his army for sixteen years, until Scipio's attempt on Carthage forced Hannibal to return to rescue his own country. There was Hannibal overthrown, and his city made to pay great reparations by Scipio, who for his victory there, was named *Africanus*.

In the third war (because the people of Carthage again broke their agreement) their city was razed to the very ground by the earnest and continual council of Cato the Elder [234-149 BC], fearing evermore so dangerous a neighbour.

Though Scipio Nasica counselled to the contrary, fearing least if the dread of that enemy were taken away, the Romans would grow either to idleness, or civil dissention; which afterwards they did.

It is reported of Cato, that he never spoke his judgement of any matter in the Senate, without concluding "…and furthermore I think that Carthage must be destroyed".

Livy reported, that the way whereby Cato prevailed, was this; while the question was very hot, he brought into the Senate house green figs, and let the Senators understand, that the same day three weeks, those figs were growing in Carthage town: whereby he made manifest to them., that it was possible that any army might be conveyed from Carthage to Rome in so short a time as that they would not be able (on a sudden) to resist, and so Rome might be surprised: whereby they all concluded, that it was no safety for their city to have a bad neighbour so near to them.

In this country toward the west, not far from Carthage, stood Utica, where the younger Cato[88] killed himself in the civil wars between Caesar and Pompey, unwilling to accept clemency from his enemy Caesar[89].

Not far from there westward, stands Hippo, which was the city where St Augustine[90] was Bishop.

This whole country (at this day) is called the kingdom of Tunis; the king whereof, is a kind of stipendiary to the Turk: the people that inhabit there are generally Saracens and do profess Mahomet.

Some do write that Tunis stands in the very place where old Carthage was; which is not so, but it is situated very near. Against the King of Tunis, Charles I[91] had some of his wars by sea.

---

[88] The great grandson of Cato the Elder, 95-46 BC.

[89] Caesar commented "Cato, I grudge you your death, as you would have grudged me the preservation of your life."

[90] Philosopher and theologian (354-430) – of Hippo, not Canterbury.

[91] That is, Charles I of Spain (1516-1556), later the Emperor Charles V.

Of Mauritania Tingitana

The other part of Barbary that lies along the Mediterranean, farthest into the west, was called in old time Mauritania Tingitana. The people of which country were those which almost in all the old histories were called by the name of Maures: those of the other Mauritania being rather termed Numidians.

Into the northwest part hereof did Hercules come, and there did set up one of his pillars, which answered to the other in Spain, they both being at the straits of Gibraltar. On the south part thereof lay the kingdom of Bocchus [King of Mauretania, c110 BC] which in the time of Marius had so much to do with the Romans. In the west part of this Mauretania stands the hill called Atlas Minor and on the south part is the great hill called Atlas Major, after which the main ocean which lies between Mauretania and America is called the Atlantic Ocean. This hill is so high, that to those who stood on the bottom of it, it seemed to touch heaven with his shoulders.

This country has been long inhabited by the Saracens, who after their finding it to be but a short passage into Spain, did go over (now 700 years ago) and possessed there the kingdom of Granada, on the south side of Spain, until they were then expelled by Ferdinand and Elizabeth, or Isabella, King and Queen of Castile. In this country since that time, have the Spaniards taken some cities and strongholds; and so also have the Portuguese: which by the divers event of victory, have often been lost and won by them.

Here it was that the Emperor Charles V, had divers of his great wars against the Moors, as well as in the kingdom of Tunis. For the assistance of one who claimed to be king of a part of this country [Abu Abdallah Mohammed II Saadi of Morocco] did Sebastian the King of Portugal go with all his power into Africa, in the year 1578 where, unadvisedly bearing himself, he was slain the same day together with two others who claimed to be kings: so that there it was that the battle was fought, whereof it was said, that three kings died in one day. Which battle of Alcazar was the ruin of the kingdom of Portugal, and the cause of the uniting it to the Crown of Spain. Astrologers did suppose that the blazing star which appeared the year before, did signify that ill event.

This whole country does maintain in it, besides some imperial government, two absolute kingdoms: the one of Fez, which lies on the north part towards the Mediterranean and Spain: the other is the kingdom of Morocco, which lies from above the hill Atlas Minor, to the south and west part of Mauretania. These are both Saracens, as be also their people; holding true league with the Turk, and with some other Christian Princes, a league only for traffic and merchandise.

It may be doubted whether it was in this Mauretania Tingitana, or near to it, in Mauretania Caesaria, of which St. Augustine in his book *De doctrina Christiana*, of his own knowledge reports, that in a city of the country was this brutish custom, that once in the year (for certain days) the inhabitants of the place did assemble themselves into wide and large fields, and there divided themselves each from other, so that perhaps the fathers were on one side, and the children or brothers on the other; and did throw stones with such violence that many were hurt, and divers killed with the fury of that assault.

But St. Augustine tells, that he, detesting the brutishness thereof, did make a most eloquent and elaborate oration or sermon to them, whereby he did prevail with those of the city where he was, that they gave over the foolish and rude exercise. Yet Leo Africanus [c. 1494-1554, Moorish diplomat, otherwise al-Hasan ibn Muhammad al-Wazzan al-Fasi], who lived about a 100 years since, and in his own person travelled over the greatest part of Africa, does write in his description of Africa, that in one place of the kingdom of Fez, the like barbarous custom is yet retained.

Of the other Countries of Africa lying near the Sea

From beyond the hill Atlas Major, to the south of Africa, is almost nothing in antiquity worthy the reading, and those things which are written (for the most part) are fables. For towards the south part of Africa, as well as towards the north parts of Europe and Asia, be supposed to be men of strange shapes, as some with dogs' heads, some without heads, and some with one foot alone, which was very huge, and such like; which that counterfeit friar (who wrote that book which pretends to be by St.Augustine, *Ad Fratres in Eremo*, and who would gladly father upon St.Augustine the erecting of the Augustinian friars) does say, that he saw travelling down from Hippo southward in Africa. But as the ass in Aesop's fables which was clothed in the lion's skin, did by his long ears show himself to be an ass, and not a lion, so this foolish fellow, by his lying, does show himself to be counterfeit, and not St.Augustine.

In the new writers there are some few things to be observed: as first, that all the people in general to the south, lying within the *Zona Torrida* [the Tropics] are not only blackish, like the Moors, but are exceedingly black, and therefore at this day they are named Negros, than whom no men are blacker.

Secondly, the inhabitants of all these parts which border on the sea coast, even unto the Cape of Good Hope, have been gentiles, adoring images and foolish shapes for their gods, neither hearing of Christ, nor believing on Mahomet. The Portuguese coming among them have professed Christ for themselves, but have won few of the people to embrace their religion.

Thirdly, that the Portuguese passing along Africa to the East Indies, have settled themselves in many places of those countries, building castles and towns for their own safety, and to keep the people in subjection, to their great commodity.

One of the first countries famous beyond Morocco, is Guinea, within the compass whereof lies Cape Verde, the Cape Three Points and the town and castle named Sierra Leone. At which place (where commonly all travellers do touch that do pass that way, for fresh water, and other ship provision) our Englishmen have found traffic into the parts of this country, where their greatest commodity is gold, and elephants' teeth; of both which there is good store.

Beyond that toward the south, not far from the Equator, lies the kingdom of Congo, where the Portuguese at their first arrival, finding the people to be heathens, without God, did induce them to a profession of Christ, and to be baptised in great abundance, accepting the principles of religion until such time as a priest could teach them to lead their lives according to their professions. The most part of them in no case enduring, they returned back again to their heathenness.

Beyond the Congo so far to the south as almost ten degrees beyond the Tropic of Capricorn, lies the land's end; which is a promontory, now called the Cape of Good Hope, which Vasco da Gama the Portuguese did discover[92], and so called it, because he had there good hope that the land did turn to the north; and that following the course thereof he might be brought to Arabia and Persia, but especially to Calicut in India.

Which course, when himself, and other of his countrymen after him did follow, they found on the coast up towards Arabia, the kingdom of Mozambique and others, whose people were all gentiles, and now are in league with the Portuguese, who have built divers strongholds for their safety. Of which countries, and manners of the people, he that wishes to read, but there is no matter of any great importance.

Beyond the Cape toward the north, before you come to Mozambique, between the rivers of Cuama and Sancto Spirito

---

[92] In fact, it was discovered by Bartolomeu Dias in 1488; he originally named it the Cape of Storms. King John II of Portugal renamed it.

[Zambesi and Limpopo], lies the kingdom of Mutapa, where also the Portuguese have arrived, and so much was done there by the preaching of Gonzalo da Sylva, a Jesuit, that the king and queen of that country with many others, were converted from heathenness to Christianity and baptised. Certain Mohammedans incensing the king thereof afterwards against the Portuguese, made him revolt from his religion, and to put to death this Jesuit and others. The Portuguese assaying to revenge, with an army sent for out of Portugal, profited little against him, but were themselves consumed by the discommodities of the country, and the distemperature of the air.

There are also other kingdoms in this part of Africa, of whom we know little besides their names, such as Adel, Monomugi, Angola, and therefore it shall be sufficient to have named them in a word.

Of Abyssinia, and the Empire of Prester John

In the inland of Africa, lies a very large country, extending itself on the east to some part of the Red Sea, on the south to the kingdom of Melinda, and a great way farther, on the north to Egypt; on the west to the Congo. The people whereof are called Abyssinians; and itself the dominion of him, whom we commonly call in English Prester John; but in Latin for the most part *Presbyter Johannes*, writing of him. As he is a prince absolute, so he has also a priest-like or patriarchal function and jurisdiction among them. This is a very mighty Prince, and reputed to be one of the greatest Emperors in the world.

What was known of this country in former time, was known under the name of Ethiopia, but the voyages of the Portuguese in these late days have best described it. The people thereof are Christians, as is also their Prince; but differing in many things from the western Church, and in no sort acknowledging any supreme prerogative of the Bishop of Rome.

It is thought that they have retained Christianity even from the time of our Saviour, being supposed to be converted by the Chamberlain of Candace the Queen of Ethiopia, who was instructed concerning Christ, by Philip the Evangelist in the Acts of the Apostles [8, 26-39]. Eusebius [Bishop and historian, c. 263-339 AD] in his Ecclesiastical History does make mention of this.

But they do to this day retain circumcision: whereof the reason may be, that the eunuch (their converter) not having any further conference with the Apostle, nor any else with him, did receive the ceremonies of the Church imperfectly retaining circumcision: which among the Jews was not abolished when he had conference with Philip.

Within the dominion of Prester John, are the mountains commonly called the Mountains of the Moon, where is the first well-spring and rising of the River Nile. Yet there are that fetch the head of this river out of a certain great lake toward the south, called Zembre [Lake Tanganyika] : out of which toward the west runs the river of Zaire [Congo], into the kingdom of the Congo. The river of Zuama [Zambesi], towards the south, to the kingdom of Monomotapa [in the modern states of Zimbabwe and Mozambique] as this river Nile towards the north, through the kingdom of the Abyssinians to Egypt, which river running violently along this country, and sometimes hastily increasing by the melting of much snow from the mountains, would overrun and drown a great part of Egypt, but that it is flaked by many ponds, dams and sluices, which are within the dominion of Prester John. In respect hereof, for the maintenance of these, the Princes of Egypt have paid to the governor of the Abyssinians a great tribute time out of mind, which of late the great Turk supposing it to be a custom needless, did deny. Until the Abyssinians by commandments of their Prince, did break down their dams, and drowning Egypt did enforce the Turk to continue his pay, and to give much money for the new making of them, very earnestly to his great charge, desiring a peace.

In this country also of Prester John is the rising of the famous river Niger, supposed to have in it the most and the best precious stones of any river in the world, after it has run a good space hid itself for the space of 60 miles under ground, then appearing again after it has run somewhat further, make a great lake, and again after a great tract, another; and at last, after a long course, falls at Cape Verde into the Atlantic Sea.

There be other countries in Africa as Agisimba [supposed to be the most southerly region of Ethiopia], Libya Interior, Nubia, and others, of whom nothing is famous: but this may be said of Africa in general, that it brings forth store of all sorts of wild beasts, as elephants, lions, panthers, tigers, and the like.

According to the proverb, *ex africa semper aliquid novi* [Pliny, slightly misquoted: "There is always something new out of Africa"].

Oft times new and strange shapes of wild beasts are brought forth there, the reason whereof is, that the country being very hot, and full of wilderness which have little water, beasts of all sorts are enforced to meet at those few watering places that be. There often contrary kinds have conjunction the one with the other, so that there arises a new kind of species, which takes part of both. Such a one is the leopard, begotten of the lion, and the [purely legendary] beast called the pard, which somewhat resembles either of them.

And thus far of Africa[93].

---

[93] The legend of Prester John was not decisively disproved until 1681, by Hiob Ludolph, a German orientalist, and the geography of central Africa was not fully established until the 19th century, by explorers such as Mungo Park and David Livingstone. The theory of evolution had not yet evolved.

Of the Northern Islands

The islands that do lie in the north, are in number almost infinite: the chief of them only shall be briefly touched. Very far to the north in the same climate almost with Sweden, that is, under the Arctic Circle, lies an island called in old time Thule[94], which was then supposed to be the farthest part of the world northward, and therefore is called by Virgil, Ultima Thule. The country is cold, the people barbarous, and yields little commodity, saving hawks. In some part of the year there is no night at all. To this land divers of our English Nation do yearly travel, and do bring from there good store of fish, but especially, our deepest and thickest ling, which are therefore called island-lings.

It hath pleased God, that in these latter times, the Gospel is there preached, and the people are instructed in Christianity, having also the knowledge of good learning, which is brought about by the means of the King of Sweden, to whom that island is now subject.

There is lately written by one of that nation a pretty treatise in Latin, which describes the manner of that country; and it is to be seen in the first tome of Master Hakluyt's *Voyages*[95].

Southward from there, lies Friesland. On the coast of Germany, one of the 17 provinces is called Zealand, which contains in it divers islands; in whom little is famous, saving that in one of them is Flushing [Vlissingen], a town of war, and Middelburg is another: a place of good mart.

The States of the Low Countries do hold this province against

---

[94] It is not entirely clear to what this refers, though both Iceland and Greenland have been suggested.
[95] *The Principal Navigations, Voiages, Traffiques and Discoueries of the English Nation* (1589-1600) by Richard Hakluyt, a churchman and a contemporary of George Abbot.

the King of Spain. These islands have been much troubled of late with inundation of water.

The island that lies most west of any fame, is Ireland, which had in it heretofore many kings of their own; but the whole land is now annexed to the Crown of England. The people naturally are rude and superstitious, the country good and fruitful, but that for want of tillage in divers places, they suffer it to grow into bogs and deserts. It is true of this country that serpents and adders do not breed there; and in the Irish timber, of certain experience, no spider's web is ever found.

The most renowned island in the world is Albion, or Britannia, which has heretofore contained in it many several kingdoms, especially in the time of the Saxons. It has now in it two kingdoms, England and Scotland, wherein are four several languages; that is, the English (which the civil Scots do barbarously speak) the Welsh tongue (which is the language of the old Britons) the Cornish (which is the proper speech of Cornwall;) and the Irish (which is spoken by those Scots which live on the west part of Scotland near to Ireland).

The commodities and pleasures of England are well known to us and many of them are expressed in this Verse:

Anglia, Mons, Pons, Fons, Ecclesia, Femina, Lana.

England is stored with Bridges, Hills, and Wool;

With Churches, Wells, and Women beautiful.

The ancient inhabitants of this land were the Britons, which were afterward driven into a corner of the country now called Wales; and it is not to be doubted, but at the first country was peopled from the continent of France, or thereabout, when the sons of Noah had spread themselves from the east to the west part of the world.

It is not strange to see why the people of that nation do labour to fetch their pedigree from one Brutus, whom they report to come from Troy; because the original of that truth began by Geoffrey of Monmouth, about 500 years ago, and his book [*The History of the Kings of Britain*, c. 1136] contains great show of truth, but was noted by William of Newburgh[96] or some author of his time, to be merely fabulous.

Besides that, many of our English nation have doubted the saying of them who would attribute the name of Britannia to Brutus, and Cornwall to Coryneus. Aeneas Sylvius [Pope Pius II] has thought good to confirm it: the English people (saith he) do report, that after Troy was overthrown, one Brutus came to them, from whom their kings do fetch their pedigrees.

We do find in ancient records and stories of this island, that since the first possessions which the Britons had here, it was overrun, and conquered several times.

The Romans were the first that did attempt upon it, under the conduct of Julius Caesar, who did only discover it, and frighted the inhabitants with the name of the Romans, but was not able so far to prevail upon it, as any way to possess it. Yet his successors afterwards did by little, and little, so gain on the country, that they had almost all of it which is now called England, and did make a great ditch or trench from the east to the west sea, between their dominion here, and Scotland. Divers of the Emperors were here in person, as Severus, who is reputed to be buried at York. Here also was Constantius, father to Constantine the Great, who from hence married Helena, a woman of this land, who was afterwards mother to the renowned Constantine.

But when the Romans had their empire much weakened, partly by their own discords and partly by that decay which the eruptions of the Goths and Vandals, and suchlike invaders did bring upon them, they were forced to retire their Legions from there, so leaving the country naked; the Scots, and certain people called the Picts, did break in, who most miserably wasted and spoiled the country. Then were the inhabitants (as some of our authors write) put to that choice, that either they must stand it out

---

[96] Who wrote in around 1190 that "it is quite clear that everything this man wrote about Arthur and his successors, or indeed about his predecessors from Vortigern onwards, was made up, partly by himself and partly by others".

and be slain, or give ground, until they came to the sea, and so be drowned.

Of these Picts, who were the second over-runners of this land some do write, that they used to cut and stamp their flesh, and lay on colours, which did make them the more terrible to be seen with the cuts of their flesh. But certain it is, that they had their name for painting themselves, which was a common thing in Britain in Caesar's time, as he reported in his commentaries, the men colouring their faces with woad, that they might seem the more dreadful, when they were to join battle.

The third sort of people which attempted upon this land were the Danes, who took advantage of the distressed state of the inhabitants here: and having obtained their purpose, not without great resistance and blood shed, did bear themselves more imperiously and tyrannically than any other before or after them,

To meet therefore with their cruelty and oppression the Saxons in the fourth place were by some of the land called in, who finding the sweetness of the soil, and commodiousness of the country every way, did repair here in great troops, and so seated themselves here, that there were soon seven several kingdoms and kings of them within the compass of England.

These Saxons did bear themselves with much more temperance and tolerance towards those few of the country that remained than the Danes had done: but yet growing to contention, one of these kings with another, partly about the bounds of their territories, and partly about other quarrels, they had many great battles each with other.

In the time of these, religion and devotion was much embraced, and divers monasteries, and rich religious houses were founded by them, partly for penance which they would do, and partly otherwise, because they thought it to be meritorious, insomuch that King Edgar alone is recorded to have built about four monasteries. And some other of their kings were in their ignorance so devoted, that they gave over their crowns, and in superstition did go to Rome, there to lead the lives of private men.

These seven kingdoms in the end, did grow all into one; and then William Duke of Normandy, pretending that he had right thereunto by the promise of adoption, or some other conveyance from Harold, did with his Normans pass over into this land, and obtained a great victory in Sussex, at a place which he caused in remembrance thereof to be called Battle. He built an Abbey there, by the name of Battle Abbey. He took on him to win the whole by conquest, and did bear himself indeed like a conqueror. For he seized all into his hands, gave out barons, lordships, and manors from himself; reversed the former laws and customs, and instituted here the manners and orders of his own country; which have proceeded on, and been by little and little bettered; so that the honourable government is established, which we now see at this day.

It is supposed, that the faith of Christ was first brought into this land in the days of the Apostles, by Joseph of Arimathea, Simon Zelotes and some other of that time. But without doubt it was found here not long after, which appears by the *Testimony* of Tertullian[97,] who lived within less than 200 years after Christ. And there are records to show, that in the days of Eleutherius, one of the ancient Bishops of Rome [c174-189 AD], King Lucius received here both baptism and the Gospel.

Insomuch that it is fabulous vanity to say, that Augustine the monk[98] was the first that here planted the Christian faith, for he lived 600 years after Christ, in the time of Gregory the Great, Bishop of Rome [and first enumerator of the Seven Deadly Sins]. Before which time, Gildas [6th century British cleric and historian] is (upon great reason) thought to have lived here; of whom there is no doubt, but that he was a learned Christian. Yes, and that may be

---

[97] Early Christian author, c160-220 AD, who wrote (not in his *Testimony*) of "all the limits of the Spains, and the diverse nations of the Gauls, and the haunts of the Britons, inaccessible to the Romans, but subjugated to Christ".

[98] St Augustine of Canterbury (Abbot refers to him as Austin) landed in 597 AD, and as the first Archbishop carried out missionary work amongst the Anglo-Saxons who had not so long before conquered a large part of England.

perceived by that which Bede [the Venerable Bede, d. 735 AD, monk, scholar and historian] has in his Ecclesiastical History concerning the coming in of Augustine, that the Christian religion had been placed here before, but that the purity of it in many places was much decayed, and also that many people in the island were yet infidels, for the conversion of whom, as also for the reforming of the other, Augustine was sent here.

Here he behaved himself so proudly, that the best of the Christians which were here did mislike him. In him was erected the Archbishopric of Canterbury, which amongst old writers is still termed Dorobernia. The Archbishops do reckon their succession by number, from this Augustine [George Abbot was number 75].

The reason wherefore Gregory the Great is reported to have such care for the conversion of the natives of Britain, was because certain young boys were brought him out of this country; which being very goodly of countenance (as our country children are therein inferior to no nation in the world) he asked them what countrymen they were; and it was replied that they were *Angli* [Angles], he said they were not unfitly so called, for they were *Non Angli sed Angeli, si forent Christiani* [Not Angles but Angels; if only they were Christians!].

And demanding further, of what province they were in this island, it was returned that they were from Deira [roughly, Yorkshire], which caused him again to repeat that word, and to say, that it was great pity, but that by being taught the Gospel they should be saved *de ira Dei* [from the wrath of God].

England has since the time of the Conquest, grown more and more in riches, insomuch that now more then 300 years ago, in the time of King Henry III, it was an ordinary speech, that for wealth, this country was *puteus inexhaustus*, a Well that could not be drawn dry.

Which conceit the King himself, as Mathew Paris [13th century Benedictine monk and chronicler] writes, did often suggest to the Pope; who thereupon took advantage, abusing the simplicity of the King, to suck out inestimable sums of money, to the intolerable grievance of both the clergy and laity. And among other things, to bring about his purpose, the Pope did persuade the King, that he would invest his young son in the Kingdom of Apulia, which did contain a great part of all Naples, and for that purpose had from him many thousands, besides infinite sums which the King was forced to pay for interest to the Pope's Italian usurers.

Since that time it has pleased God more and more to bless this land, but never more plentifully than in the days of our late, and now reigning Sovereign[99], whose reign continuing long in peace, has peopled the land with abundance of inhabitants, has stored it with shipping, armour, and munition, has fortified it many ways, has increased the traffic with the Turk and Muscovite, and many parts of the earth far distant from us, has much bettered it with building, and enriched it with gold and silver. It is now (by wise men) supposed, that there is more plate within the kingdom, then there was silver when Her Majesty came to the Crown.

Some writers of former times, yes, and those of our own country too, have reported that in England have been mines of gold, or at the least some gold taken out of other mines: which report has in it no credit, in as much as the country stands too cold, neither has it sufficient force of the sun to concoct and digest that metal[100]. But truth it is that our chronicles do witness, that some silver has been taken up in the southern parts, as in the tin mines of Devonshire and Cornwall, and such is sometimes found now but the virtue thereof is so thin that by that time it is tried and perfectly fined, it does hardly quit the cost: notwithstanding, lead, iron and such baser metals, be here in good plenty.

The same reason, which hinders gold ore from being in these parts, that is to say, the cold of the climate, does also hinder that there is no wine, whose grapes grow here. For although we have grapes, which in the hotter and warm summers do prove good, but

---

[99] Abbot's work was first published in the reign of Elizabeth I, but subsequent editions were brought out under James I and Charles I.
[100] In fact nearly all British gold mines have been in Wales.

yet many times are nipped with the frost before they be ripe, yet notwithstanding they never come to that concocted maturity as to make sweet and pleasant wine. Yet some have laboured to bring this about, therefore have planted vineyards to their great cost and trouble helping and aiding the soil by the uttermost diligence they could; but in the end it has proved to very little purpose.

The most rich commodity which our land has naturally growing is wool, for the which it is renowned over a great part of the earth. For our clothes are sent into Turkey, Venice, Italy, Barbary, yes, as far as China of late, besides Muscovy, Denmark, and other northern nations. For the which we have exchange of much other merchandise necessary for us here. Besides that, the use of this wool does in several labours set many thousands of our people in work at home, which might otherwise be idle.

Amongst the commendations of England is the store of good bridges: whereof the most famous are London Bridge and that at Rochester. In divers places here, there be also rivers of good name, but the greatest glory does rest in three, the Thames, the Severn and Trent, which is commonly reputed to have his name of trente, the French word signifying thirty, which some have expounded to be so given, because 30 several rivers do run into the same. Some others do take it to be so called, because there be 30 several sorts of fishes in that water to be found; the names whereof do appear in certain old verses recited by Mr Camden, in his Book of the Description of England[101].

One of the honourable commendations which are reputed to be in this Realm, is the fairness of our greater and larger churches, which as it does yet appear in those which we call cathedral churches, many of them being of very goodly and sumptuous buildings. So in times past it was more to be seen, when the abbeys, and those which were called religious houses, did flourish, whereof there were a very great number in this kingdom, which did eat up much of the wealth of the land. But those which lived

---

[101] William Camden's *Britannia*, first published in 1586.

there, giving themselves to much filthiness, and divers sorts of uncleanliness, did so draw down the vengeance of God upon those places, that they were not only dissolved, but almost utterly defaced by King Henry VIII. There are here two Archbishops, and 24 other Bishops within England and Wales.

It was a tradition among old writers, that Britain did breed no wolves in it, neither would they live here. But the report was fabulous, inasmuch as our chronicles do write, that there were here such store of them, that the kings were enforced to lay it as an imposition upon the kings of Wales, who were not able to pay much money for tribute, that they should yearly bring in certain hundreds of wolves; by which means they were at the length quite rid from wolves.

The country of Wales had in times past a king of itself, yes, and sometimes two, the one of north Wales, and the other of south Wales; between which people at this day, there is no great good affection: But the kings of England did by little and little so gain upon them, that they subdued the whole country to themselves, and in the end King Henry VIII, intending thereby to benefit this realm and them, did divide the country into shires, appointed there his judges of the circuit and by Act of Parliament, made them as capable as any other subjects of preferment in England.

When the first news was brought to Rome that Julius Caesar had attempted upon Britain, Tully in the elegance of his wit (as appears in one of his Epistles) did throw scorn at it, saying that there was no gain to be gotten by it. For gold here was none, nor any other commodity to be had, unless it were slaves, whom he thought that his friend to whom he wrote would not look to be brought up in learning or music[102]. But if Tully were alive at this day, he would say, that the case is much altered, inasmuch as in our nation is sweetness of behaviour, abundance of learning, music, and all the liberal arts, goodly buildings, sumptuous apparel, rich fare, and what forever else may be truly boasted to be

---

[102] Cicero, *Letters to Atticus* 4.16.7

in any country near adjoining.

The northern part of Britain is Scotland, which is a kingdom of itself, and has been so from very ancient time, without any such conquest, or main transmutation of state, as has been in other countries. It is compassed about with the sea on all sides saving where is joins upon England; and it is generally divided into two parts, the one whereof is called the Highlands and the other the Lowlands.

The Lowlands are the most civil part of the Realm, wherein religion is more orderly established, and yields reasonable subjection to the King: but the other part, called the Highlands, which lies further to the north, or else bends towards Ireland, is more rude and savage and whither the King has not so good access, by reason of rocks and mountains, as to bring the noblemen which inhabit there, to such due conformity of religion as he would.

This country generally is more poor than England, or the most part of the kingdoms of Europe, but yet of late years, the wealth thereof is much increased by reason of their great traffic to all the parts of Christendom. Yes, to Spain itself, which has of late years been denied to the English and some other nations, and yet to this day they have not any ships, but for merchandise, neither has the King in his whole dominion, any vessel called a man of war. Some that have travelled into the northern parts of Scotland, do report, that in the summer solstice they have scant any night, and that which is, is not above two hours, being rather a dimness then a darkness.

The language of the country is in the Lowland, a kind of barbarous English. But towards the Ireland side, they speak Irish: which is the true reason whereof it is reported, that in Britain there are four languages spoken, that is Irish in part of Scotland, English for the greatest part: Welsh in Wales; and Cornish in Cornwall.

In the confines between the two kingdoms of England and Scotland, which are commonly called the Borders, there lie divers outlaws and unruly people; which as being subject to neither prince by their good wills, but so far as they list, do exercise great robberies, and stealing of cattle from them that dwell thereabout: and yet the princes of both realms, for the better preservation of peace and justice, do appoint certain Wardens on each side, who have power, even by martial law, to repress all enormities.

The Queen of England had on her side three, whereof one is called the Lord Warden of the East Marches, the other of the West Marches, the third, the Warden of the Middle Marches, who with all their power cannot so order things, but that by reason of the outrages thereabouts committed, the borders are much unpeopled; while such as desire to be civil, do not like to live in so dangerous a place.

It has been wondered at by many that are wise, how it could be that whereas so many countries, having in them divers kingdoms and rulers, did all in the end come under the dominion of one (as appears at this day in Spain, where were wont to be divers kings, and so in times past in England – where the seven kingdoms of the Saxons did grow all into one) yet that England and Scotland, being continuous within one island, could never until now be reduced to one monarchy. In reason the French may be thought to have been the greatest hindrance. For they, having felt so much smart by the armies of England alone, insomuch that sometime all that whole country almost has been overrun and possessed by the English, have thought that it would be impossible that they should resist the force of them, if both their kingdoms were united and joined into one.

The customs therefore of the kings of France in former times was, that by their gold they did bind to them the kings and nobility of Scotland, and by that means, the kings of England were no sooner attempting anything upon France, but the Scots by and by would invade England. Whereupon the Proverb amongst our people grew, that He who will France, win, must with Scotland first begin.

And these Frenchmen continuing their policy, did with infinite rewards break off the marriage which was intended and agreed upon between King Edward VI, and Mary the late unfortunate Queen of Scotland[103], drawing her rather to be married with the Dauphin of France, who was son to King Henry II, and afterward himself reigned by the name of King Francis II. But this was so ill taken by the English, that they fought revenge upon Scotland, and gave them a great overthrow in that battle which was called Musselburgh field[104].

The people of this country were in times past so barbarous, that they did not refuse to eat man's flesh: which as Saint Jerome [Christian writer, 4th century AD] does witness of them, he himself saw some of them to do in France[105], and the news of the same thereof went so far, that Chrysostom [St John Chrysostom, d 407 AD] in one place does allude to such a matter.

There be many little islands adjoining to the great island of Britain: as at the very north point of Scotland are the Orkney islands, which are in number about 30 and whereof the people are barbarous.

On the west side of Scotland towards Ireland, lie the islands called Hebrides, in number 44, where inhabit the people ordinarily called the redshanks[106]. Not far from there, is the isle Mona, commonly called the isle of Man, the peculiar jurisdiction of the Earls of Derby[107], with homage notwithstanding reserved to the Crown of England.

On the north part of Wales, is the island of Anglesey, which is reputed a distinct Shire.

Towards France, on the south part of England is the Isle of

---

[103] By the Treaty of Greenwich, in 1543; in 1587 Mary Queen of Scots was executed on the orders of her nearly-sister-in-law, Elizabeth I.

[104] Or more commonly Pinkie Cleugh (1547), part of the campaign described as The Rough Wooing.

[105] Apparently a scurrilous misattribution of atrocities perpetrated by Scythian tribes.

[106] Not all Hebrideans, but short-term mercenary soldiers from the Western isles, so called because they went bare-legged, with kilts.

[107] Whose (Stanley) family had been given the island by Henry IV.

Wight, in Latin called *Vectis*, which is a good stronghold in the narrow seas against the French. Nearer France are the isles of Guernsey and Jersey, where they speak French, and are under the Crown of England. There are also many other, but of small account: as the isles of Thanet and Sheppey on the side of Kent, the Scilly islands at the end of Cornwall, in number as it is said 145, Caldey, Lundy, and the Flat Holme, with others in the mouth of the Severn, Holy island and the Farnes, and Coquet island on the side of Northumberland.

And thus much of Great Britain, and the islands thereto adjoining.

Of the Islands in the Mediterranean Sea

There be many islands in the Mediterranean, renowned in all the old writers: but the chief of them only shall be touched. From the Pillars of Hercules going eastward, are two islands not far from Spain, which are called the Balearic islands, for that the people of them did use (both for their delight and armour) slings[108], which they continually (almost) carried about with them.

Whereto, as Pliny writes, they did train up their children from their youngest years, not giving them any meat, until they had from some post or beam cast it down with a sling. These were the sling casters, which the Carthaginians and Spaniards did use in their wars against the Romans.

The lesser of the islands, which lies most west is called Minorca: the bigger, which lies more east, is called Majorca, and they are both under the dominion of the King of Spain.

More eastward in the Tyrrhenian Sea lies the island of Corsica, over against Genoa: and direct southward from there lies the great island of Sardinia. For the quiet possession of which two, the wars were often revived between the old Carthaginians and the Romans, for these two islands lie in the middle very fitly.

The island of Corsica is subject to the state of Genoa, and is ruled by their Governors, as the Venetians do Crete. This island is but barren compared to some others that lie near to it, or to the country of Italy; but yet it yields profit, ease, and honour to Genoa, which has little land beside it.

The island of Sardinia also is no way so fruitful as Sicily, but it is under the government of the King of Spain, and was the same which was promised to Anthony the King of Navarre, father to Henry IV, King of France, in recompense of Pamplona and the rest

---

[108] The name of the islands was thought to derive from Greek *balliareis*, or slingers.

of the kingdom of Navarre then, and now, detained from him and his heirs, by the Spaniard. But this was the device only of the Cardinal of Lorraine, who intending to draw him to Papistry, and to order his politic purposes, did make show of this, which was no way meant by the Spaniard.

Further to the east, at the very point of the south part of Italy lies the great island of Sicily, which some have supposed to have been heretofore a part of the continent: but by an earthquake and inundation of water to have been rent off, and so made an island. The figure of this country is triangular.

There was a great contention for this country, between the Carthaginians and the Romans, but the Romans obtained it, and had from there exceeding store of corn yearly, whereupon Sicily was called the Granary of the Roman People. Here stood the goodly city called Syracuse, which was destroyed and sacked by Marcellus the Roman[109]. Livy writes of him that he, being resolved to set on fire that city, which was then one of the goodliest places of the world, could not choose but break forth into tears, to see how vain and transitory the glory of worldly things is here.

At that time lived Archimedes, who was a most admirable ingenious engine maker for all kind of fortifications, of whom it is said, that by burning glasses which he made, he did set on fire divers ships which the Romans had lying in the harbour. When the city was taken, he was making plans, and drawing figures on the ground, to prevent the assault of the Romans, and being unknown, he was slain by some of the soldiers, which did break in upon him. Some think that it was he, and not Archytas [428 BC – 347BC, philosopher and polymath] who made the dove, of which it is written that it was so equally poised, that being thrown up into the air, it would hover or flutter there, and in a good space not fall down.

This was in times past a kingdom, where the two tyrants, the

---

[109] The Consul Marcus Claudius Marcellus took the city after a three year siege, in 214 BC.

elder and the younger Dionysius did reign [4th century BC], where Gelo also, that great friend to the Romans did rule [5th century BC].

It was afterward made a province, and governed by a Praetor of the Romans: whereof Verres was one, who was so inveighed against by Tully[110].

It grew afterward to be a kingdom again, insomuch that Tancred was king of Sicily, which entertained our Richard I, when with Philip the King of France, he went to the conquest of the Holy Land[111]. Here was likewise Phalaris the tyrant so famous[112], king of Agrigentum.

The tyrannies which were used in Sicily were in times past so famous that they grew into the proverb "Envy - No greater torment was devised by Sicilian tyrants". But they who were the causes of all, did often speed very ill themselves: as appears by the elder Dionysius, who being driven out of his dominion, did flee into Italy, and was glad there to teach children, that so he might supply his necessity.

His son grew more tyrannous then the father, and stood so far in fear of his own people, that many times he caused himself to be shut up in a tower, and set his guard to keep the door, that nobody might come at him. He dare not trust his barber to shave or clip him, for fear of cutting his throat; but that which was done he caused his daughters to do, who with the thin inner skin of walnuts being set on fire, is said to have taken off the hair off his face.

This was he who when Damocles, a flatterer, did seem marvellously to admire his felicity, caused him to be set one day at dinner for as royal feast, with dainty fare before him, fine plate,

---

[110] Gaius Verres was prosecuted by Cicero in 70 BC for corruption in this office; Verres fled into exile before the end of the trial and his oratory brought fame and advancement for Cicero.

[111] In 1190-91; "entertained" is not quite the right word; Richard's forces sacked Messina and enforced his demands on Tancred.

[112] Tyrant from 570 to 554 BC. He was famous for his cruelty and his cannibalistic inclinations.

rich hangings, music, and all other matters of delight - but withal a naked sword, which was only tied with a single hair of a horse's mane, to be hanged directly over him. The fear whereof did so fright the flatterer, lest it should fall upon him, that he continually looked upwards, and about him, and took no joy of that which was before him. Whereby Dionysius did evidently teach him, that the state of some princes, howsoever it seem glorious to others, yet it does bring little contentment to themselves, by reason of the continual dangers which hang over them.

It is reported of his man, that when all the people of his country did for his cruelty continually curse him, there was one women which daily did go to the churches, and prayed the gods to lengthen his life. When he was acquainted of this, marvelling at the reason of it, he sent for her, and asked what good thing he had done to her, that she was so careful ever more to pray for him?

But the woman answered, that it was not for love, but for fear that she begged these things of the gods. For (said she) "I am an old woman; I do remember when your grandfather lived, who being very hard to his people, was much maligned by them, and they prayed that they might be rid of him. Which falling out, afterward your father came in place, and he was worse than the former: which when the subjects could not endure, they prayed also that he might die, hoping that the next would be better. Then came yourself in place, who have much exceeded the cruelty of your father; and whereas others wish that you were gone also, trusting for amendment in the next, I that have lived so long, and see that things grow worse and worse, do pray that you may continue, because that if we should have one that should succeed you, if he walk in the steps of his predecessors, he must need be as bad as the Devil himself; for none else in tyranny can go beyond you".

Phalaris of Agrigentum was he who proposed rewards to him who invented new torments, which caused Perillos to make a bull of brass, into the which if offenders should be put, and fire should be set under, then it would make them roar like a bull. But when upon the terror thereof none would so offend (as to deserve that torment) Phalaris took Perillos, the author thereof, and to try the experience, put him into it, whereby he lost his life.

This country is now also under the King of Spain, who among other titles, was wont to call himself King of both Sicilies, reckoning this island for one: and that part of Italy for another which is now called Calabria, and was in the Roman histories named Greater Greece.

There is nothing more renowned in all Sicily, either with new or old writers, then Mount Etna: which being on the outside often covered with snow, yet by a sulphurous or brimstony matter, does continually burn within. Yes, so that whereas it was supposed in the age last before us, that the matter being consumed, the fire had ceased: twice in our age it has broken forth again, to the incredible loss of all the country adjoining, the ashes therefore destroying vines and fruits, which were within the compass of many miles about.

The reason of this fire approved both by historians and philosophers is, that within the ground, there is great store of sulphur and brimstone matter, which having once fire in it, is apt to keep it. And whereas all the whole country is full of chinks and chaps, and hollowness within the ground, the matter which enters there, does minister substance to the continuance of that flame: as we see that water cast on coals in the smith's forge, does make them burn more fervently: and then into the chinks and chaps, the wind does also enter, which by blowing and whistling, does both cause the fire never to extinguish, and sometimes (according to the strength of the blast) does make flames break out, either more or less.

There are in the hill Etna, two principal places which are like to two furnaces, with tunnels on the top of them, where divers times, (but especially in the evening and night) the flame does appear, mounting upwards; and it is so strong, that often it brings up with it burnt and scorching stones, and pieces of hard substances, which seems to be rent out of some rock, to the great terror and danger of any that do come near.

This is that place where Empedocles[113] threw himself, that he might be reported a god.

This is it whereof Virgil does make his tract called *Aetna*[114,] and which the poets did report to be the workshop of Vulcan, where the Cyclopes did frame the thunderbolts for Jupiter.

And to conclude, that is it, which some of our gross Papists have not feared to imagine to be the place of Purgatory, as they have been so foolish to think, that there is also another place called the Mount Veda in Iceland, where souls have another Purgatory to be punished in; but there by cold, which Surius[115] in his commentaries is so absurdly gross as to report and allow.

The Papists have shown for their Purgatory in Etna, out of that book which is commonly called by the name of the *Dialogues of Gregory the Great*, for in that book there are divers things to that purpose. But our best writers of late, have discovered that that same treatise is a counterfeit, being made by a latter Pope Gregory, and not by the first of that name, ordinarily called Gregory the Great[116,] who although he has in his works divers things tending to superstition, yet he was never so absurd as to write things so improbable, foolish, and grounded upon so bare reports as these were.

Such another hill as the Mountain of Etna is, was in time past Vesuvius, a hill in Campania, which is part of Italy. But this never had the like continuance as that of Etna[117], although in the time of Pliny, the fire did break forth there, and so strongly, as that the elder Pliny, who spent all his time in discovering the secrets of nature, pressing near to behold it, was stifled with the flame, smoke or ashes. So that he died in the place, as is most excellently

---

[113] Philosopher of 5th century BC; Diogenes Laertius (3rd century AD) records this story.

[114] Not now generally held to be by Virgil; the authorship is doubtful.

[115] Laurentius Surius, 16th century Carthusian hagiologist.

[116] This work now seems to be accepted as genuine.

[117] Vesuvius lay dormant from the end of the 13th century until it erupted with great force in 1631.

described in the Book of his Epistles by his nephew the young Pliny.

Not far from Sicily, on the south lies the little isle called Malta. This is the place where St. Paul was cast up after his ship wrecked in his journey to Rome, where the viper hanged on his hand, and did not hurt him.

This country is one of the places most renowned in the world for repelling of the Turks: When Suleiman the Emperor of them, did send against it a most mighty army [in 1565], it was then defended by the Knights of Malta, which by sea do great spoil to the galleys of the Turk that pass that way.

There were in times past divers Orders of Knights, and men that had vowed themselves to adventure their lives and whole estate for the maintenance of Christ's religion and some places of the earth against the infidels and Saracens.

The most ancient of all those, were called the Templars, who were a great corporation or society, consisting of divers gentlemen, younger brothers for the most part, out of all the Realms of Christendom: Their chief charge was to defend the city of Jerusalem, and the relics or remainder of the Temple there, and Sepulchre of Christ: for the preservation of which places, together with the rest of the Holy land, they had given to them, and purchased for their money, very rich and ample possessions in England, France, Spain, Italy, and other places of Europe, in so much that in the days of Matthew Paris [13th century], he reported that they had under them many thousands of manors.

They had also in every kingdom (where their Order was permitted) a great and ample house, where some chief of their company did lie, who received the rents within that kingdom, and caused the money to be transported into the Holy Land, and other ordinances to be made and executed belonging to their Order. Of which houses, the Temple that is now in London was a chief one; which had in former times belonged to the Jews, but was afterwards translated to that use. When the Holy Land was quite taken by Saladin, and could never be recovered into the hands of the Christians, the society of these Temples ceased, the Pope and the King of France conspiring their ruins [at the beginning of the 14th century], and their lands were dispersed into divers men's hands.

In the same time when the Templars were in their strength, there was another sort called Hospitallers, whose condition and employment was very like to the other, both of them fighting for the preservation of Palestine.

We read that sometimes these two companies had great jars [quarrels] between themselves, whereby grew much hindrance to the wars against the infidels.

All these were accounted as orders of religion, and therefore it was forbidden them at any time to marry, without dispensation from the Pope; because not being entangled to wife and children, they might be resolute to adventure their lives.

After them grew up the order of the Knights of Rhodes, who since they could not live in the Holy Land, yet would abide as near to it as possible they might. And therefore, partly to preserve pilgrims which would go to visit the Sepulchre of Christ, and partly to trouble the Turks and Saracens, but especially to keep the enemies of Christ's faith from encroaching further upon Christendom, which most earnestly they did, and do desire, they placed themselves in the islands of Rhodes, where daily doing great hurt to the Turk, Suleiman the great warrior could not endure them, but with a mighty army so overlaid them, that he won the island from them [in 1522].

After the loss of Rhodes, the island of Malta was given to these Knights by the Emperor Charles V, whereupon they are now called the Knights of Malta. For the Great Master after he came from Rhodes, went into Crete, and from there into Sicily, and so into Italy, from there he made a voyage into England, and then into France, and lastly into Savoy, from where he departed with his Order into this island, and there they continue and behave themselves as in the former island. Offering no violence to Christians, they much hinder the courses of the Turks from Greece and Asia, and other Saracens from Fez and Morocco. They are very valiant men, fit to do great service, either by land or sea as appeared when Suleiman did think to have surprised them and their island: the description of which war is diligently laid down by Caelius Secundus Curio [moderate reformer, a contemporary of Calvin], in a treatise dedicated to Elizabeth Queen of England.

There have been divers other orders of knights, in Portugal, France, England, Burgundy, and some other places of Christendom; but because their service has not been employed purposely, as these which are before mentioned, we do not touch them in this place.

Near to Greece and the Peloponnese, on the west side towards Italy, is the isle of Corfu, and not far south from that, is Kefalonia; and from there south, is Zakynthos. All which islands are at this day under the Venetians.

The greatest commodity which that country does yield, are currants, which are gathered of a kind of small grape. For the making whereof, they commonly one time every summer, for the space of three weeks, have a continual drought, day and night, in which time, the currants are laid abroad in the open air, and may not be taken in. Insomuch, that if the season do continue hot and dry, their merchandise is very good: but if there fall any rain until the time be expired of their full drying, the currants are not good, but do mould and change their colour to be somewhat white, like meat. The state of Venice, under whom this island is, does make a great commodity of the impost, or taxation, which is laid upon this merchandise, calling the tribute which is paid for them, the Revenue of Saint Mark: for to that Saint is the city of Venice dedicated, and they hold him for their Patron.

In this island (besides the merchants who repair there) are divers Italians, who be there in garrison for the Venetians; in one special castle, which commands the whole island.

There are also divers Friars of that nation; who perform to their countrymen such exercises of religion as are convenient. They will not suffer any of our merchants to have Christian burial among them, unless at his death he be confessed after the Romish fashion: whereupon some have been forced to convey over some of their dead bodies into Morea, (which is not far distant) to be buried there among the Greeks, and after their fashion.

The natural inhabitants of Zakynthos are Greeks, both by language and religion, and observe all fashions of the Greek Church: in whose words (being now much corrupted and depraved) there may yet be found some tokens and remainders of the old, pure, and uncorrupted Greek.

There are in this country great store of swine kept, whereof the inhabitants do feed, and carry them into Morea; but the Turks there (by their Mahometan profession) will taste no swine's flesh.

In Zakynthos our English merchants have a dwelling house for their business. South east from Morea lies the great island Crete, where Minos, so famous for his severity, some time did reign.

This country was then called Hecatompoleis, as having in it 100 towns and cities. Here stood the labyrinth which was the work of Daedalus, who designed it so by the manifold turnings, infiniteness of pillars and doors, that it was impossible to find the way; yet Theseus (by the help of Ariadne the daughter of king Minos) taking a reel of thread, and tying the one end at the first door, did enter and slay the Minotaur, which was kept there, and afterwards returned safe out again.

The ancient inhabitants of this country were such noted liars, that the Apostle Paul in his Epistle to Titus, who was left there by him as Bishop of that island, does cite a verse out of the heathen Poet Epimenides, that the Cretans are ever liars, evil beasts, and slow bellies [Titus 1.12].

This island is in our days called Candy, being the place from where our sugar of candy is brought. It is under the Venetians, and reputed a part of their empire. The Turk, when they had taken Cyprus, did think also to have surprised it: but that it pleased God by the means of Don John of Austria, in the behalf of his brother the King of Spain, and the Venetians, to give the Turk that great overthrow at sea, in the fight near to Lepanto. Yet since that time (no doubt) the Turks have a greedy eye upon the island of Candy.

Between Crete and the Peloponnese, lies Kythira. There was the fine Temple of Venus, who therefore by the poets is called Citherea. The islands are many which lie in the Aegean Sea, from the bottom of Greece, to the top of the Hellespont, as all the Cyclades, Euboea, and the great islands Samos, and Chios; also Skyros where Achilles was born, and was king of that country[118].

There is also Lesbos and Ithaca, where Ulysses was king, and Andros, where Themistocles[119] was sent by the Athenians to collect tribute, as Plutarch tells. Themistocles did tell them that he came to demand tribute, or some great imposition upon them, being accompanied with two goddesses, the one was Eloquence to persuade them; and the other, Violence, to enforce them. Whereto the Andreans made answer, that they had on their side two goddesses as strong, whereof the one was Necessity whereby they had it not; and the other was Impossibility, whereby they could not part with that which they never possessed.

Of these places, something may be read in the old history of the Greeks. Divers of these did strive that Homer was born in them; but of certain many of those kings which Homer said came with Agamemnon to the siege of Troy, were kings but of those small islands.

Eastward from there, not far from some part of Anatolia, or Asia Minor, is the island of Rhodes, the friendship of the inhabitants whereof was in ancient time very much desired, so that Alexander first, and the Romans afterwards, did embrace their league.

Here was that huge and mighty image of the sun, which was

---

[118] Skyros was according to mythology where his mother sent Achilles, disguised as a girl, to avoid being conscripted for the Trojan War, until he was detected by Odysseus (Ulysses); he was not its king.

[119] Eminent Athenian politician and general, who played a great part in the defeat of the Persian invasion by Xerxes in the 5th century BC.

called the Colossus of Rhodes[120.]

This country was long defended by those who were called the Knights of Rhodes, against the power of the Turk, and it was a great bulwark to defend Christendom, until that in the year 1521, Suleiman the great Turk, did win it from the Christians by force.

From there southward is the isle Karpathos: but in the farthest end of the east part of the Mediterranean, is Cyprus, which about 300 years since, was a kingdom, and did afford great aid to the Christians that went to conquer the Holy Land; but it is now under the Turk. The chief city thereof is Famagusta, which is an Archbishop's see: for Christians, by paying their tribute, do yet live there. In this country in old time was Venus much honoured, and therefore she was called Cypria, as also Paphia, because she had a Temple in a city there called Paphos.

Near to Syria stood the island of Tyre, against the pride whereof, the Prophets do much speak. This was a rich city for merchandize and navigation in old time, and is the place from where Dido, and the builders of Carthage did come.

The destruction of it is most famous by Alexander the Great. Of the rest of the small islands we do say nothing.

---

[120] One of the Seven Wonders of the World, it was a statue of the sun god, Helios, built in the 3rd century BC.

Of the Islands in the Indian Sea

The islands are very many that do lie in the seas adjoining to the East Indies; but only the most famous amongst them shall be touched. Among old writers was well known that which was then called Taprobana, which lies near the Equinoctial Line[121]. It was in that time a monarchy where the kings reigned not by succession, but by election: and if any of them did grow intolerable, he was deposed and enforced to die, by withdrawing from him all things necessary. This is now called Sumatra, and has in it divers kings.

Not far from thence lie eastward the two islands called Java Major and Java Minor[122], which were also known to the old writers, as in general may be noted, that all the east part either in the continent, or in the islands, have very many small kings and kingdoms.

From where yet more east, lies a great number of isles, which are now called the Moluccas[123], which are places as rich for their quantity as any in the world; from these it is that the Spaniards have yearly so great quantity of all kinds of spice, neither is there any place of all the East Indies, that does more richly furnish home their carracks, than do these Moluccas.

The islands which are called by that name are by some of our writers accounted to be at least four and twenty or five and twenty [apparently nearly 1000]; and some of them which are the bigger, have in them two or three kings apiece: and some of them which are less, are either the several dominions of several kings, or else

---

[121] An imaginary line encircling the Earth, everywhere equally distant from the two poles.

[122] It seems that Abbot's Java Major was modern Java, whereas Java Minor was Sumatra.

[123] Now the Maluku islands, historically the Spice Islands.

two or three of them do belong to some one prince. When Sir Francis Drake did encompass the whole world, he came near to these, but did not touch at any of them; but Master Candish [Thomas Cavendish, 1560-1592] taking as large a journey, was in one or more of them, where he found the people to be intelligent and subtle, and the kings of the country to take upon them as great state as might be convenient for such petty princes.

Some of these islands the Spaniards through the Portuguese have got into their own possession, with the kings of some other they have leagued; and a third sort utterly detest them. More northward over against China, lies a country consisting of a great many islands [nearly 7000] called Japan, the people whereof are much of the same nature with the men of China: this country was first discovered by the Jesuits, who in a blind zeal have travelled into the farthest parts of the world to win men to their religion. This island is thought to be very rich.

About the parts of Japan, there are divers people, whose most ordinary habitations is at the sea, and do never come into the land, but only for their necessities, or to furnish themselves with new vessels, wherein they may abide; but lying not far from the land, they have ducks, and other fowls swimming about them, which sometimes they take into their boats and ships, and in such sort do breed them, to the maintenance of them and their children.

Into this Japan of late days have our English also sailed, as into other parts of the East Indies, and there erected a factory [a centre for trading].

The rest that be either near to Asia or Africa, because there is little written of them, we pass over, only naming them, as the Philippines, Borneo: as also on the side of Africa, the island of Saint Laurence, called by the inhabitants of Madagascar, and other of less note. It was known in old time, that there were many islands near to the East Indies, which were first discovered by the trafficking of the islanders into the continent; so no doubt that navy which Alexander sent out to India to descry and cruise through the eastern seas, did give much light thereunto, partly by that which themselves did see, and partly by those things which they heard in such places, or of such persons as they met with in their travel.

Of the Islands in the Atlantic Sea

There be many islands which be westward from Africa and from Europe: as those which are called the Gorgades [the islands of Cape Verde], that lie in the same climate with Guinea, which are four in number, not inhabitated by men, but they are full of goats. Northward from thence, in the same climate with the south part of Morocco, lie those which are called the Canaries, or the Fortunate Islands, which are seven in number: being most fruitful and very pleasant, and therefore called by that name. This is famous in them, that it has pleased all cosmographers to make their meridian to be their first point where they do begin to reckon the computation of their longitude, and to them after three hundred and three score degrees to return again.[124]

From these islands it is, that those strong and pleasant sacks [white fortified wines], which are called Canary wines are brought; and from there are fetched those that they call Canary birds. These islands are under the Crown of Spain: the heat of the country is very great, and therefore fitter for concoction, but besides that the soil of itself is accommodated thereunto, and by reason of them, both these islands do bring forth a grape, which is sweeter in taste then any other grape, and has that property with it, that the wine which is made thereof, does not fume into the head, like other sack, but does help the stomach, and exercise the force of it there. The slips of their vines have been brought into Spain and some other places of Europe, but they have not sorted to the same purpose, as they do in their native country.

---

[124] The current site of the Prime Meridian was not established until 1884, when at an international conference held in Washington DC a resolution fixing the Meridian at Greenwich was passed 22-1 : San Domingo voted against, France and Brazil abstained. The Canary Islands are now regarded as being 15°24'W.

There do grow also in these isles, good store of sugar canes, which yield plentifully that kind of commodity, to Spain, either for marmelets[125] (wherein they much delight) or for other uses.

On the backside of Africa is the Isle of Saint Thomas, inhabited by the Portuguese; which island was taken in the latter time of Queen Elizabeth by the Dutch. It is reported that in the midst of this island is a hill, and over that a continual cloud, wherewith the whole island is watered, (such a like thing as this is reported of the Isle of Cloves [Zanzibar]). The air of this island is unwholesome, and there is hardly seen any Portuguese or stranger that comes to dwell there who lives until he be about 40 years of age.

More northward from Africa lie those islands which are called the Azores, being six or seven in number: of which Terceira is one of the chief: of whom, the rest by some are called Terceiras, which are far inferior in fruitfulness to the Canaries. These were first under the Crown of Portugal, and one of them was the last which was kept out from the King of Spain, by the Prior Don Antonio[126], who afterward called himself King of Portugal. But the Spaniard at last took this Terceira from him, and does possess all these islands, together with the rest of the dominion which did belong to the Portuguese.

Who wishes to see the unadvised proceedings of Don Antonio both in parting with Lisbon, and the rest of Portugal, as also in losing these islands which last of all held out for him, let him read Conestágio's[127] book on the union of Portugal with the Crown of Castile.

Now they are the place where the Spaniards do commonly touch, and take in fresh water, both going and coming to and from America, finding that to pass directly without turning on either hand towards America is very hard, by reason of the strong

---

[125] A sort of solidified fruit paste, used as confectionery.

[126] 1531-1595; King Antonio I of Portugal for 33 days in 1580, then claimant to the Portuguese throne occupied by Philip II of Spain.

[127] Jerome Conestágio (died 1635), Genoese historian, diplomat and Archbishop of Capua.

current of the water from the Gulf of Mexico, and so forward to the east. So therefore they are enforced either to go lower to the south, and so to water in some part of Guinea, or thereabout, or else to keep up as high as these islands.

Of America, or the New World

Although some do dispute out of Plato and the old writers, that there was not only a guess, but a kind of knowledge in ancient time, that besides Europe, Asia, and Africa, there was another large country lying to the west, yet he that shall advisedly peruse the conjectures made thereupon, may see that there is nothing of sufficiency to enforce any such knowledge, but that all antiquity was utterly ignorant of the new found countries towards the west.

Whereunto this one argument most forcible may give credit, that at the first arriving of the Spaniards there, they found in those places, nothing showing traffic, or knowledge of any other nation; but the people naked, uncivil, some of them devourers of men's flesh, ignorant of shipping, without all kind of learning, having no remembrance of history or writing among them; never having heard of any such religion as in other places of the world is known, but being utterly ignorant of Scripture, or Christ, or Moses, or any God, neither having among them any token of cross, church, temple, or devotion, agreeing with other nations.

The reasons which are gathered by some late writers out of Plato, Seneca, and some other of the ancient, are rather conjectural, that it was likely that there should be some such place, then any way demonstrative, or concluding by experience, that there was any such country: and the greatest inducement which they had to persuade themselves that there was any more land towards the west then that which was formerly known, was grounded upon this, that all Asia, Europe, and Africa, concerning the longitude of the world, did contain in them but 180 degrees: and therefore it was most probably, that in the other 180 which filled up the whole course of the sun to the number of 360 degrees, God would not suffer the water only to possess all, but would leave a place for the habitation of men, beasts, flying and creeping creatures.

I am not ignorant that some, who make too much of vain shows, out of the British antiquities, have given out to the world, and written something to that purpose, that Arthur, sometime King of Britain, had both knowledge of these parts, and some dominion in them.

For they find (as some report) that King Arthur had under his government many islands, and great countries, towards the north and west, which one of some special note has interpreted to signify America, and the northern parts thereof, and thereupon have gone about to entitle the Queen of England to be sovereign of those provinces, by right of descent from King Arthur.

But the wisdom of our state has been such, as to neglect that opinion, imagining it to be grounded upon fabulous foundations, as many things are which are now reported of King Arthur; only this does carry some show with it, that now some hundred of years since, there was a knight of Wales, who with shipping and some pretty company, did go to discover those parts, whereof as there is some record of reasonable credit amongst the monuments of Wales. So there is this one thing which gives pregnant show thereunto, that in the late navigation of some of our men of Norumbega[128], and some other northern parts of America, they find some tokens of civility and Christian religion. But especially they do meet with some words of the Welsh language, as that a bird with a white head should be called pengwinn, and other such like. Yet because we have no invincible certainty hereof, and if anything were done, was only in the northern and worse parts, and the intercourse between Wales and those parts, in the space of divers hundred years, was not continued, but quite silenced, we may go forward with that opinion, that these western Indies were no way known to former ages.

God, therefore, remembering the prophecy of his Son, that the Gospel of the Kingdom should before the day of judgment, be preached in all coasts and quarters of the world, and in his mercy

---

[128] A legendary town believed to have existed in north-eastern America.

intending to free the people, or at the least some few of them, from the bondage of Satan (who did detain them in blockish ignorance) and from their idolatrous service to certain vile spirits (whom they call their *Zemes*, and most obsequiously did adore them), raised up the spirit of a man worthy of perpetual memory, one Christopher Columbus, born at Genoa in Italy, to set his mind to the discovery of a new world.

Who, finding by that compass of the old known world, that there must needs be a much more mighty space (to the which the sun by his daily motion did compass about) then that which was already known and discovered; and conceiving that this huge quantity might as well be land as sea, he could never satisfy himself until he might attempt to make proof of the verity thereof.

Being therefore himself a private man, and of more virtue then nobility, after his reasons and demonstrations laid down, whereby he might induce men that it was no vain thing which he went about: he went to many of the princes of Christendom, and among others to Henry VII, King of England, desiring to be furnished with shipping and men fit for such a navigation. But these men refused him, partly because they gave no credit to his narration; and partly lest they should be derided by their neighbour princes, if by this Genoese stranger they should be cousoned [misled]; but especially, for that they were unwilling to sustain the charges of shipping.

At last he took himself to the Court of Ferdinand and Isabella, King and Queen of Castile, where also at the first he found but small entertainment, yet persisting in his purpose without weariness, and with great importunity, it pleased God to move the mind of Queen Isabella, to deal with her husband to furnish forth two ships for discovery only, and not for conquest. Whereupon Columbus, in the year 1492, accompanied with his brother Bartholomew, and many Spaniards, sailed far to the west, for the space of 300 days and more, with the great indignation and often mutinies of his company, fearing that by reason of their long distance from home, they should never return again. Insomuch that the general, after many persuasions of them to go forward, was at length enforced to crave but three days, wherein if they saw not the land, he promised to return.

And God did so bless him, to the end that his voyage might not prove in vain, that in that space, one of his company did spy fire, which was a certain argument that they were near to the land; as it fell out indeed.

The first land whereto they came, was an Island, called by the inhabitants Haiti, but in remembrance of Spain from whence he came, he termed it Hispaniola [*La Isla Española* – the Spanish island]: and finding it to be a country full of pleasure and having in it abundance of gold and pearl, he proceeded further, and discovered another big isle, which is called Cuba, of the which being very glad, with great treasure he returned to Spain, bringing joyful news of his happy success.

When Columbus did promise to restrain the time of their expectation within the compass of three days, engaging himself to return if in that space they saw no land; there be some write, that he limited himself not at all at risk, but that he did by his eye discern a difference in the colour of the clouds which did arise out of the west, from those which formerly he had seen. Which clouds did argue by the clearness of them, that they did not arise immediately out of the sea, but that they had passed over some good space of the land, and thereby grew clearer and clearer, not having in them any or late risen vapours; but this is but conjectural.

The Spaniards, who are by nature a people proud, have since the death of Columbus laboured to obscure his fame, envying that an Italian or stranger should be reported to be the first discoverer of those parts.

And therefore have in their writings since, given forth that there was a Spaniard which had first been there and that Columbus meeting with his descriptions, did but pursue his enterprise, and assume the glory to himself.

But this fable of theirs does savour of the same spirit wherewithal many of them in his lifetime did reproach him, that it

126

was no matter of importance to find out these countries, but that, if that he had not done it, many other might, and would. Which being spoken to Columbus at a solemn dinner, he called for an egg, and willed all the guests one after another to set it up on end. Which when they could not do, he, gently bruising the one end of it, did make it flat, and so set it up, by imitation whereof each of the other did the same; whereby he mildly did reprove their envy towards him and showed how easy it was to do that which a man had seen done before.

To go forward therefore: Columbus being returned to Castile, after his welcome by the Princes, was made Great Admiral of Spain, and with a new fleet of more ships was sent to search further, which he accordingly did, and quickly found the mainland, not far from the Tropic of Cancer.

Which part of the country, in honour of Spain, he called *Hispania Nova* [New Spain]; in respect whereof at this day the King of Spain does entitle himself *Hispaniarum Rex*[129].

Some there be which write, that Columbus did not discover further then the islands; and that he spent the greatest part of his former labours in coasting Cuba and Hispaniola, to see whether they were islands, or a continent; and that some other in the mean time did thrust themselves forward and descried the firm land; Among whom Amerigo Vespucci [1454-1512] was the chief, from whose name a great part of the country is called at this day America.

They found the people both of the mainland and islands very many in number, naked, without clothes or armour; sowing no corn, but making their bread of a kind of root, which they call maize. Men most ignorant of all kind of learning, admired the Christians as if they had been sent down from Heaven, and thought them to be immortal, wondering at their ships, and the tackle thereof. For they had no ships of their own, but big troughs,

---

[129] "King of all the Spains" – but this description had been used as early as 1080 to mark rulers of more than one of the diverse Spanish kingdoms.

which they call their canoes, being made hollow (of the body of a tree) with the sharp bones of fishes, for iron or such like instruments they have none.

Although it does appear, that by the wars of one of their petty princes, or kings, had against another, many thousands of the inhabitants of those countries, where continually wasted and spoiled: yet the number of them was so great in every part of the West Indies, that in Hispaniola alone, there were supposed to be by computation of the Spaniards (first arriving there) not so few as two million, which yet by the cruelty of the Spaniards were so murdered, and in other ways made away, that within 50 years after, as their writers report, there were scant any thousands in that island remaining of them.

The like is to be said of the populousness of other coasts and quarters there.

The armour which those people did wear when they entered into the wars was nothing but some slight covering, either made of wood or shells of fishes, or of cotton wool, or some such foolish matter. For they had no use at all of iron or steel; but the most part of them came without any kind of clothing, or covering, yet armed with bows and arrows, which were made sharp in the end with the scraping of fish bones, or with fish bones themselves put on the end like an arrow head; and that often they dipped in a kind of most venomous poison. Some other of them had for the weapons great clubs, wherewith they did use to beat out the brains of those with whom they did combat.

They had amongst them no good nor wholesome food, for even that maize whereof they made their bread, had in the root thereof a most venomous kind of liquor, which is no better than deadly poison, but they crush out that juice, and afterward do prepare the root, so that it makes them a kind of bread.

There was no sort of good literature to be found amongst them, they could not so much as distinguish any times, the one from the other, but by a blockish kind of observation of the course of the Moon: according to which they made their computation, but without any kind of certainty, saving for some few months which were lately past. For the set calculating of aught which was done several years before, they could do nothing therein but only grossly aim at.

In all ages it has appeared that Satan has used ignorance as one of the chiefest means whereby to increase idolatry, and consequently to enlarge his kingdom; it were otherwise incredible, that any who have in them reason, and the shape of men, should be so brutishly ignorant of all kind of true religion, devotion, and understanding.

For the adoration which they do give, was only to certain foul spirits, which they call by the name of their *Zemes*. In remembrance of whom, divers of them did keep in their houses certain things made of cotton wool, in the manner of puppets, or like children's' babies [dolls], and to these they did yield a reverence, supposing some Divine nature to be in them, because sometimes in the evening and in the night time they had such illusions offered to them, as that they saw these their puppets to move and stir up and down in the houses, and sometimes to utter voices, and give divers significations of such things as they would have to be done, or not to be done. Yes, and that with such effect from the devil also, that if their wills, and commandments were not fulfilled, there was some vengeance or punishments executed upon them or their children, the more to keep them in awe and servility, to the great Enemy of mankind.

Not long after the Spaniards entered those parts, there were in divers of the islands, and some part of the mainland, such incredible tempests and disturbances of the air, by wind and rain, thunder and lightning, as that the like had never been seen nor heard of in the memory of man. These are ordinarily interpreted to be the special work of the Devil, who not unfitly is termed by Saint Paul the Prince of the Air, as having a liberty given him of God, there sometimes to do strange works.

Of likelihood, he did make these stirs, either grieving that the name of Christ was at all brought into those parts, or else seeking to fright the inhabitants from associating themselves with those who brought (although but superstitiously) the knowledge of God, and the Redeemer, being desirous that they should expect more such distemperatures and vexations, if they would confederate themselves with them.

The people were so ignorant of all human and civil conversation, and trafficking into those parts, at the first coming of the Christians there, that they thought they could never sufficiently admire their persons, their shipping or any other thing which they brought with them.

Whereupon they without ceasing gazed on the manner of their ships, seeing them to be so great, and consisting of divers planks. But they were never satisfied with staring upon their masts, sails, cables, and other ropes and tackle, whereto they had never beheld anything like before. Yet nature and necessity had taught them to make to themselves certain vessels for the sea, of some one tree, which they get down, not with cutting, but with fire: and when it lay along upon the ground, they did use also fire, either to burn away that which was tough and unfit without, or to make it hollow within: although they have also the shells and bones of fishes, whereby they made smooth.

But some of these troughs or canoes were so great that sometimes above 20 men have been found rowing in one.

The trees of America, but especially in Brazil, are so huge that it is reported of them that several families have lived in several arms of one tree, to such a number as are in some petty village or parish in Christendom.

Among other strange opinions, which they conceived of the Spaniards, this was one, that they were the sons of some god, and not born of mortal seed, but sent down from Heaven to them: and this conceit was the stronger in them because at the first, in such conflicts as they had with them, they could kill few or none of them. The reason whereof was partly the armour of the Spaniards, and partly the want of iron and steel upon the arrows which the Americans did shoot. But they were not very long of that opinion that they were immortal, but reformed their error, both by seeing the dead corpses of some of the Christians, and by trying an experiment upon some of them also, for they took them, and put their heads under the water, and held them until they were choked. By which they knew them to be of the same nature as other men.

Among other points which did show the great ignorance, and unlettered stupidity of these Indians, this was one, that they could not conceive the force of writing of letters. Insomuch that when one Spaniard would send to another, being distant in place, a letter, the poor Indian would marvel how it should be possible that he to whom the letter came should be able to know all things which the sender directed. And thereupon divers of them did think that there was some kind of spirit in the paper, and marvellously stood in fear of such a thing as a letter was.

This country yielded great abundance of strange herbs, the like whereof are not to be found in others parts of the world, as also some very rare beasts, as one among the rest, who by description, has some part like an elephant, some part like a horse, and divers others parts like divers other beasts; nature having studied to express a great many several creatures in one.

There are also found at the sea, or within some rivers, crocodiles [as we now know, alligators], but not of that hugeness as those that breed in Egypt, in the River Nile, whereof some are described to be at the least 24 cubits [roughly 20 metres] in length, which argues the crocodile to be the greatest creature in the world that comes of an egg.

There are also thereabouts, some extraordinary stones growing in the land, such as the blood-stones, whereof there are great store: but especially there is one thing of great beauty and worth, that, the abundance of pearls, which are taken in shell fishes. They are of as great a quantity as any that be in the seas near to the East Indies, so that the true cause of the plenty of pearl in Europe, in this our age, incomparably beyond that which has been in the days of our forefathers, is to be ascribed to the discovery of these new found lands.

There are also here divers trees which are not to be found elsewhere: and many roots, which serve for divers purposes.

Among other things (whereof there is great plenty in those western parts) is the abundance of kine [cattle]: whereof they report, that there is such store in Cuba and Hispaniola, that there are killed several thousands every year, whereof the Spaniard makes no other use, but to take the tallow, or the hide. This serves them in their shipping, and for divers other purposes, but the flesh of the most part of them, they suffer for to putrefy, as making little account of it, partly because of the heat of the country, wherein they eat little flesh, and partly because they have great store of hens, and other more dainty meat, whereupon, together with fish, they do very much feed.

It may seem a kind of miracle to him who looks no higher then the ordinary rules of nature, and does not respect the extraordinary and unlimited power of God, that whereas a great part of America does lie within the Tropics, in the self same climate with Ethiopia, and the hottest parts of the East Indies, where the inhabitants are not only tawny, as all be in Egypt, and in Mauritania, but also coal black, and true negroes, here there is no man whose colour is black, except it be those which are brought out of Africa. The people are of a reasonable fair complexion: which is to be ascribed only to God's peculiar will, and not to that which some foolishly have imagined, that the generative seed of those people should be white, and that other of the Ethiopians black; for that is untrue, inasmuch as the Ethiopians' case does not differ from the quality of other men.

The Spaniards did find the people here to be most simple, without fraud, giving them kind entertainment, according to their best manner; exchanging for knives and glasses, and such like toys, great abundance of gold and pearl.

It is certain, that by the very light of nature, and by the ordinary course of human shape, there were among this people very many good things, such as affability, in their way, hospitality towards strangers who had not offended them, according to their ability, and open and plain behaviour.

Yes, and in some parts of these West Indies there was an opinion that the soul was immortal, and that there was life after this life: where beyond certain hills (they know not where) those which died in defence of their country, should after their departure from this life, remain in much blessedness. Which opinion caused them to bear themselves very valiantly in their fights, either striving to conquer their enemies, or with very good contentment enduring death (if it were their hap to be taken, or slain) in as much as they promised themselves a better reward elsewhere. But withal, as it could not choose but be so, there were many other grievous sins amongst them, such as adoration of devils, sodomy, incest, and all kind of adultery: ambition in very high measure; a deadly hatred each to other: which proceeded all from the fountain of ignorance wherewith Satan had blinded their eyes. There were among them some which by a kind of blind witchcraft, had to evil purpose, acquaintance and intercourse with soul spirits.

The manner of their attire, or beautifying themselves which divers of these people had severally in several parts did seem very strange to them who came first into that country. For some of them did adorn themselves with the shells of fishes, some did wear feathers about their heads, some had whole garments made of feathers, and those very curiously wrought, and placed together of divers colours: to which purpose they did most use the feathers of peacocks, or parrots, or such other birds whose covering was of divers colours.

Yes, in very many places they had their lower lips bored through with a great hole, and something put into them, as also into the upper parts of their ears, being pierced in like manner: which as it seemed in themselves to be a point of beauty, so it made them appear to other men to be wonderfully ugly.

The quantity of gold and silver which was found in those parts was incredible, which is the true reason wherefore all things in Christendom do serve to be sold at a higher rate then they were in the days of our forefathers. For it is the plenty of gold and silver which is brought from this America that makes money to be in greater store, and so may more easily be given then it could be in the days of our predecessors[130].

But as for the thing itself, it is testified by all writers that there were in those parts very great mines of the most precious metals and that in the banks of rivers, with the washing of the water, there was divers times revealed very good and big pieces of gold, which without melting or refining was of reasonable perfection; and the like was to be found in many places of the land when the people did dig for their husbandry, or for any other purpose.

This made the inhabitants there to account gold and silver, for the commonness of it, but as a vile thing, and yet by the reason of the colour of it, for variety's sake, to be mingled with the pearl, and worn about their necks and about their arms. And yet we do find that in some part of the West Indies, the kings did make some reckoning of gold, and by fire did make it to the best perfection, as may appear by Atahualpa[131], who had a great house piled upon the sides with great wedges of gold ready wrought, which he gave to the Spaniards for a ransom of his life, and yet they most perfidiously did take his life from him.

But the mean account ordinarily which the people had of gold, did cause them very readily to bring to the Spaniards at their first arrival, great store of that metal which they very readily exchanged for the meanest trifles, and gee-gaws, which the other could bring, even such things as wherewith children do use to play. But there was nothing more acceptable to them than axes and hammers, knives, and all tools of iron, whereof they rather make account to cut down their timber, to frame it and to do other such necessaries, to their convenient use belonging, then to fight, or to do hurt each to the other.

---

[130] In other words, this influx of precious metal was thought to be the cause of the European inflation of the 16th and 17th centuries.

[131] 1497-1533, last sovereign of the Inca Empire of South America.

And therein may appear the great variety of God's disposition of his creatures here and there; when in all that main continent of America, but especially in that which lies between or near the Tropics, there is no iron or steel to be found, which without doubt gave great way to the conquest of the strongest places there, as of Mexico by name, when armed men with guns, and other instruments of war, were to fight against them which were little better than naked, and it was rightly upbraided by one of his countrymen to Cortez[132] upon one of his returns from America, having made exceeding boast of his great victories in those parts, and coming afterwards in service into Africa, where he being hardly laid to by the Moors, and showing no valour at all, it was remembered to him, that it was an easy thing for him to do all those exploits which he cracked so much of in the West Indies, inasmuch as the people there had nothing to resist.

There was nothing more dreadful to those unarmed men than the sight of horses and men riding upon them, whereof a very few did quickly overbear many thousands of them, even almost in the beginning of the discovery of those parts.

Ferdinand and Isabella, then King and Queen of Castile, and after them Charles V, the Emperor, who succeeded them, partly to stir up their subjects to action, and partly to procure to themselves the more treasure with less expense and trouble of their own, did give leave to divers of their subjects, that by special commission they might pass into those parts, and there have several quarters and countries allotted to them. There they might dig and try out gold and silver, on condition that they did allow clear to the King the first part of such commodities as did arise to them. Therefore near to every mine and furnace the King had his special officers, who did daily attend and take up his tribute. And to the end that all things might the better be ordered, both there and in Spain

---

[132] Hernán Cortés de Monroy y Pizarro (1485-1547) leader of an expedition which between 1519 and 1521 conquered the Aztec empire and brought Mexico under Spanish rule.

(concerning the affairs of those countries) the King caused a Council, and Council house, to be newly created at Seville, where all things should be handled that did grow to any controversy and where the intelligences which should from time to time be brought out of America might be laid up as in a place of record.

The desire of gain caused the Spaniards to seek further into the countries: but the tyranny and the covetousness of the Spaniards was such, in taking from them their goods, in deflowering their wives and daughters; but especially, in forcing them to labour in their gold mines without measure, as if they had been beasts, that the people detesting them, and the name of Christians for their sakes, did some of them kill themselves, and the mothers destroyed their children in their bellies, that they might not be born to serve so hateful a nation. Some of them did in war conspire against them, so that by slaughter and otherwise, the people of the country are almost all wasted now within a hundred years, being before many millions[133]: and those which remain are as slaves, and the Spaniards almost only do inhabit those parts.

It is not unknown to all the parts of Europe, that the insolency of the Spaniards is very great, even over Christians, tyrannising and playing all outrages wheresoever they get men in subjection, and this makes them so hateful to the Portuguese at home, to the Italians in Milan and Naples, but especially to those in the Low Countries, who have therefore much desired to shake off the yoke of their governor. Besides that, they are men immoderately given to the lust of the flesh, making no conscience (even at home) even to get bastards in their young days, and reputing it no infamy to them to frequent harlots and brothel houses. But when they are abroad, especially in warlike services, they are very outrageous, impudently and openly deflowering men's wives and daughters. It may easily then be guessed, what disorder they kept in the West Indies, where the countries are hot, and the women were not able

---

[133] It seems that the original populations fell by some 90%; many of these deaths were caused by exposure to diseases which had been unknown in the Americas.

to resist their insolencies, and how they did tyrannise over the poor unarmed people, making them to drudge for them, not only like slaves, but brute beasts.

Which gross oversight of theirs, was at the first so apparent, that all of good minds did complain thereof, as appears by writings to the Pope, and other Princes, much deploring the ill usage of them who in name were Christians, towards those simple infidels. And certainly, it caused many of them to blaspheme the name of God, and of Christ, and to renounce their baptism whereto they were either forced or entreated, when they measured the God of the Christians by the actions of his servants, whom they found to be blasphemers and swearers, riotous and great drunkards, ravenous, tyrannous and oppressors, insatiable, covetous, fornicators, beyond measure given to incredible wantonness, and exercising even among themselves all kind of envy, contention, murders, poisonings, and all sort of inhuman behaviour.

Not long after the arrival of the Spaniards there, there were certain friars and religious men, who, moved with some zeal to draw the people there to the Christian faith, did travel into those parts, that so they might spread abroad the Gospel of Christ. When they came there, beholding the intemperance of their countrymen, which turned many away from the profession of religion, they were much moved in their hearts, and some of them by writings and some other of them by travelling personally back again into Spain, did inform the King and his Court, how dishonourable a thing it was to the name of Christ, that the poor people should be so abused, and how improbable it was that, those courses being continued, any of them would hardily embrace the faith.

The earnest petition of the these caused Charles V, the Emperor and King of Spain, by his edict and open proclamation published in the West Indies, to give liberty to the inhabitants and naturals of the place, that they should be in state of free men, and not of bond: but his subjects were so inured proudly to domineer over them, that this did little amend the condition of the people.

Since these days (notwithstanding) the blind zeal of the

Spaniards has been such, as that the kings have been at some cost, and other men also have been at great charge to erect divers monasteries and religious houses there, and many have taken the pains to go out of Europe, as they think for Christ's sake, to reside as monks and friars in America.

There be established some bishoprics there, and other governments ecclesiastical; and the Mass is there published, and Latin service, according to the custom of the Church of Rome, labouring to root out their infidelity but mingling the Christian religion with much Popish superstition.

By reason that the country is exceeding rich and fruitful, the Spaniards with great desire did spread themselves towards the north, where they found some more resistance, although nothing in comparison of warriors, but the greatest of their labour was, to conquer the Kingdom of Mexico; which Mexico[134] is a city very great, and as populous almost as any in the world, standing in the middle of great marsh or fen. The conqueror of this [in 1521] was Cortez, so much renowned in Spain to this day.

If there were anything at all in these West Indies which might favour of civility, or any orderly kind of government, it was in the Kingdom of Mexico: where it appeared to the Spaniards, that there is a certain settled state, which was kept within compass by some decrees and customs of their own, and which was able to make some resistance (as it may be termed) if it be compared with the other inhabitants of America, although little, if it be conferred with the forces of Christendom. But the policy of the Spaniards was, that by private means they came to understand of a King that confined near upon Mexico, who as he was of good strength, so was he of exceeding malice towards these his borderers, and by his forces and intelligence, Cortez and his company came to have their will upon Mexico.

In this country there stands a very great lake, which at the one end is very large and almost round; but towards the other end

---

[134] Tenochtitlan, the ruins of which form the foundations of Mexico City.

does contract itself again into a narrow room, and then spreads wide again and round, only about the third part of the compass of the greater end. In the lesser of the two, there are set some houses in four or five several places, which represent our villages: but in the greater part of the lake stands Mexico itself, being a city built of brick, to a good and elegant proportion, where the water issues into divers streets of it, as it is in Venice, and from some part whereof there are divers bridges to the mainland, made also of brick: but from the other sides men do come by boats, whereof there is abundant store continually going in that lake.

The writers do record, that there is to be found in this city abundance of all kind of provision, but especially fruits, and other delightful things, which are brought in from other parts of the country.

This was the chief city of all those quarters, before the arrival of the Spaniards there, and in subjection thereto were many large provinces, extending themselves every way, so that the King of this place, was a prince of great estate. Accordingly the Spaniards at this day have made it their chief and royal city, where the King keeps his Viceroy of Mexico for the West Indies, as he has his Viceroy at Goa for the East Indies: but from there have all the parts of America (but especially that which they call New Spain) their directions, and hence they fetch their laws, ordinances, and determinations, unless it be such great causes as are thought fit to be referred to the Council of Spain.

The sea which confines nearest to this city is called the Gulf of Mexico: where, as in divers other bays or gulfs, the stream or current is such that ships cannot pass directly to and fro, but especially out of the Gulf, but they are forced to take their course either high to the north, or low the south.

In the sea coasts of all this New Spain, the Kings of Spain have built many towns and castles, and therein have erected divers furnaces and forges for refining of their gold.

They that do write of the discovery of the West Indies, do report, that when Columbus at the first went there, in his

139

company's greatest distraction and doubtfulness of mind, whether to go forward or backward, and after Columbus had begged only two or three days respite, there was one of them, who, after the sea manner, going up to discover the land, did spy some fire. For the which, that being so happy and lucky a token, he did hope to receive at the hands of the King of Spain, some bountiful rewards: but when he returned home, there was nothing at all given to him, which he took with such malcontentedness and disdain, that he fled over into Africa, and there among the Moors, did renounce the Christian faith, so that he became a Saracen.

Of the parts of America towards the North

The rumour of the discovery of these parts being blown over Christendom, and the great quantity of the land together with the fruitfulness thereof, being reported abroad, some other nations did enterprise to set foot therein: as namely the Frenchmen, who sent certain ships to a part of this country, lying north from New Spain some few degrees outside the Tropic of Cancer. Into which when they had arrived, because of the continual greenness of the ground and trees (as if it had been a perpetual spring) they called it Florida: where after some few of them had for a time settled themselves, the Spaniards took notice of it, and being unwilling to endure any such neighbours, they came suddenly on them and most cruelly slew them all, without taking any ransom. And the French in revenge of this deed of the Spaniards, came in again afterwards into this country, and slew those that were the slayers of their countrymen. Yet the Spaniards, for want of men, are not able to inhabit that country, but leave it to the old people [the original inhabitants - not the high proportion of the current population who are aged over 65!].

The French had built in Florida a fort which they called Fort Caroline, and had reasonably assured themselves for their defence against the natives: but some malicious spirits amongst them fled to the Spaniards, with whom they returned again [in 1564] into Florida to the murder and overthrow of their own countrymen.

He who sees both the attempt of the Frenchmen for the inhabiting of that part, and the usage of the Spaniards towards them shall find both the covetous and insatiable nature of the Spaniards; who would not endure the French near to them, although there was land sufficient, and much to spare for both of them; also their perfidiousness in breaking of oaths and promises, and their unchristian cruelty, whereby they massacred all.

The Spaniards also, to the number of three hundred foot, and two horse, under the leadership of Ferdinando de Sota, entered Florida about the year of the Lord 1550 and there conquered a thousand miles wide and large, and after four or five years continuance in that country, took themselves again from there, and went to New Spain, landing in ships and vessels that they had built in Florida. And in all that time notwithstanding many conflicts with the natives, and divers discommodities and wants which they sustained in the country, they lost but two hundred men.

After this departure of the Spaniards out of Florida, brought there by Ferdinando de Sota, who died in the country: after the defeat of the French, and their revenge again taken on the Spaniards, the King of Spain sent there some small forces to take possession of the country, and set down there, for no other end as it is thought, but to keep out other nations from entering there. The one half whereof landed on the River of Saint Augustine, and the other half a dozen leagues from there, to the northward, at a place by them called Saint Helena.

In the year 1586 Sir Francis Drake came coasting along from Cartagena, a city in the mainland which he took after he departed from Santo Domingo, where the mortality that was amongst our English had made them to give over their enterprise to go to Nombre de Dios, and so over land to Panama to seize treasure. He was on the coast of Florida, in the height of thirty [Florida stretches from 24°27' N to 31° N]. Our men described on the shore a place built like a beacon, which was made for men to discover to seaward: so coming to the shore, they marched along the riverside, until they came to a fort built all of whole trees, which the Spaniards called the Fort of Saint John , where the King entertained half his forces that he then had in the country, which were 150 soldiers: the like number being at Saint Helena, all of them under the government of Pedro Melendez, nephew to the Admiral Melendez, that a fifteen or sixteen years before had attacked our

English in the bay of Mexico[135], this fort our English took, and not far from there the town also of Saint Augustine upon the same river, where resolving to undertake also the enterprise of Saint Helena, when they came to the haven's mouth, where they should enter, they durst not for the dangerous shoals: wherefore they forsook the place, coasting along to Virginia, where they took in Mr Ralph Lane and his company, and so came into England as you shall hear when we speak of Virginia.

In these northern parts of America, but especially within the main continent, some have written (but how truly I cannot tell) that there is a sea, which has no intercourse at all with the ocean: so that if there be any third place beside the Caspian Sea and the Dead Sea in Palestine which retained in itself great saltness and yet mingles not with the other seas, it is in these countries.

There is also in New Spain a great salt lake, as big or bigger than the Dead Sea of Palestine, in the midst of which stands the great city of Tenochtitlan, or Mexico, the mistress or imperial city of those parts, and on the banks or sides of that lake, many other cities also beside, which though they are but little in comparison of the greatness of Tenochtitlan, yet of themselves are great. This Tenochtitlan is supposed to consist of 60,000 houses, and standing in the midst and centre of this salt lake, go which way you will from the continent to the city, it is at least a league and an half or two leagues, on the lake to it. The lake, though it be in the midst of the land, ebbs and flows like the sea, and yet is 70 leagues distant from the sea.

But certain it is, that towards the south of these parts, which is the northern part of New Spain, about Mexico, there is a burning hill, which often breaks out into flames, as Vesuvius in Campania did in the time of the elder Pliny, and as Etna has done many ages since and before.

---

[135] Admiral Melendez had broken his word and attacked the fleet of John Hawkins in the harbour of Mexico; the wording of this passage suggests that it was copied directly from an account by Walter Bigges, London 1589.

It is said that eight leagues from Tenochtitlan or Mexico is a hill called by the inhabitants Popocatepetl, as much as to say, a smoky mountain, at the top whereof there is a hole of a league and a half wide, out of which are cast fire and stones, with whirlwinds; and that the thickness of the ashes lying about the hill is very great. It is reported also of this hill, that the flames and ashes thereof often destroy the fields and gardens thereabouts.

When Cortes went by it, he sent ten Spaniards, with guides of the country, to see and make report therefore to him, two of which ten venturing further than the rest, saw the mouth of this fiery gulf at the hill's top, and had they not happily soon returned towards their fellows, and sheltered themselves under a rock on the side of the hill, such a multitude of stones were cast out with the flame, that by no means could they have escaped.

The Englishmen also, desirous by navigation to add something to their own country, as before time they had travelled towards the farthest north part of America, lately finding that part which lies between Florida and New France was not inhabited by any Christians, and was a land fruitful and fit to plant in, they sent there two several times, two several companies, as colonies to inhabit that part, which in remembrance of the virginity of their Queen, they called Virginia. But this voyage being enterprised upon by private men, and being not thoroughly followed by the state, the possession of this Virginia, for that time was discontinued, and the country left to the old inhabitants.

There were some English people, who after they had understood the calmness of the climate, and goodness of the soil, did upon the instigation of some gentlemen of England, voluntarily offer themselves, even with their wives and children, to go into those parts to inhabit; but when the most of them came there (upon some occasions) they returned home again the first time, which caused that the second year, there was a great company transported there, who were provided of many necessaries, and continued there over a whole winter, under the guiding of Mr Lane[136].

But not finding any sustenance in the country which could well brook with their nature, and being too meanly provided of corn and victuals from England, they had like to have perished with famine, and therefore thought themselves happy when Sir Francis Drake, coming that way from the West Indies, would take them into his ships, and bring them home into their native country. Yet some there were of those English, which being left behind, ranged up and down the country (and hovering about the sea coast) made means at last (after their enduring much misery) by some Christian ships to be brought back again into England.

While they were there inhabiting, there were some children born and baptized in those parts, and they might well have endured the country, if they might have had such strength as to keep off the inhabitants from troubling them in tilling the ground, and reaping such corn as they would have sowed.

Again, in the days of our now reigning sovereign, in the year of Our Lord 1606, the English planted themselves in Virginia, where they do to this day continue, and have built three towns and forts, as namely Jamestown, Fort Henry[137] and Fort Charles[138], with others, which they hold and inhabit, sure retreats for them against the force of the natives and reasonable secured places against any power that may come against them by sea.

In the same height [latitude], but a good distance from the coast of Virginia, lies the island called by the Spaniards, La Bermuda, but by our English the Summer Islands[139], which of late is inhabited also by our countrymen.

Northward from them on the coast, lies Norumbega, which is

---

[136] Sir Ralph Lane, 1530-1603, Governor of Roanoke Island, Virginia, 1585-1586.

[137] Built in 1610, with a garrison of fifteen; replaced by a fort of the same name in a different location, in 1645.

[138] The first of three places which were to bear this name.

[139] In fact the Somers Isles, named after Sir George Somers, who claimed the islands for the Crown when shipwrecked on them in 1609, an episode which may have given Shakespeare an idea for *The Tempest* (1611).

the south part of that which the Frenchmen did, without disturbance of any Christian, for a time possess. For the Frenchmen did discover a large part of America, towards the Arctic Circle, and did build there some towns, and named it New France, after their own country.

As our Englishmen have adventured very far for the discovery of new found lands, so with very great labour and diligence they attempted to look for something higher than New France: and therefore with some ships they did pass there, and entered upon the land, from where they brought some of the people, whose countenance was very tawny, and dusky. This comes not by any heat, but the great cold of the climate, chilling and pricking them: but the digestion and stomach of these people is very good, insomuch that like to the Tartars and some other northern nations, their feeding was (for the most part) upon raw meat, their manners otherwise being barbarous, and suitable to their diet.

They had little leathern boats, wherein they would fish near the brink of the sea, and at their pleasure would carry them from place to place on their backs.

Notwithstanding all their pains there taken, it was a great error and ignorance in our men, when they supposed that they should find good store of gold mines in those quarters: for the country is so cold that it is not possible to find there any full concoction of the sun, to breed and work such a metal within the ground; and therefore howsoever they brought home some store of earth, which they supposed to be ore, and of shining stones, yet when it came to the trial, it proved to be nothing worth, but verified the proverb, All is not Gold that glitters.

In very many parts of these northern countries of America, there is very fit and opportune fishing, some pretty way within the sea, and therefore divers nations of Europe, do yearly send fishers there, with shipping and great store of salt: where when they have taken fish and dried it, and salted it at the land, they bring it home into Christendom, and utter it commonly by the name of Newfoundland fish.

The English about the year 1570 did adventure far for to open the north parts of America, and sailed as far as the very Arctic Circle, hoping to have found a passage by the north to the Moluccas, and to China, which hitherto neither by the north of Asia, nor by the north of America could be effected by them, by reason of the very great cold and ice in the climate.

The rest of the island [i.e. America] (being a huge space of Earth) has not hitherto, by any Christian, to any purpose been discovered, but by those near the sea coast it may be gathered, that they all which do there inhabit, are men rude and uncivil, without the knowledge of God. Yet on the northwest part of America, some of our Englishmen going through the straights of Magellan, and passing towards the north by New Spain, have touched on a country where they have found good entertainment, and the King therefore yielded himself to the subjection of the Queen of England: whereupon they termed it Nova Albion[140].

Sir Francis Drake, who touched upon that country, and for some pretty time had his abode there, does report in his voyage, that the country is very good, yielding much store of divers fruits, delightful both to the eye and taste: and that the people are apt enough by hospitality to yield favour and entertainment to strangers: but it is added withal, that they are marvellously addicted to witchcraft, and adoration of devils; from which they could not be persuaded to abstain, even in the very presence of our countrymen.

---

[140] During his circumnavigation of the globe (1577–1580), Sir Francis Drake landed on the western coast of North America and claimed an area, possibly in modern California, for Queen Elizabeth I as New Albion.

Of Peru and Brazil

When the Portuguese had first begun their navigation by Africa into the East Indies, some of them, intending to have held their course eastward to the Cape of Good Hope, were driven so far westward by tempest, that they landed in a large and great country, which by a general name is called Brazil. There they began to trade, and with towns and castles to plant themselves, before the Spanish had discovered Peru, which is the southern part of America. So that now, whatsoever the King of Spain has in Brazil, is by right of the Crown of Portugal.

When the Spaniards towards the west, and the Portuguese towards the east, had discovered many new found lands, there grew great contention between them, which should be appropriated to the one, and which might be seized on by the other. Therefore, for the better establishing of peace amongst them, they both went to Alexander VI, who was Pope in the year 1492, and somewhat before, and after: and he taking on him (after the proud manner of the Bishops of Rome) to dispose of that which belonged not to him, did set down an order between them, which was, that all the degrees of longitude (being 360 in the globe) being divided into two parts, the Spaniards should take one, and the Portuguese the other. So that in this division they were to begin in those degrees, under which some of Peru stands; from the which they, counting forwards towards the east, did allow Brazil, and 180 degrees to the Portuguese eastward, and so from Brazil westward to the Spaniards as many: so that he had in his share all America except Brazil.

This country is large, having in it many people, and several kingdoms, which are not all possessed by the Portuguese; but so, that other Christians, as namely the Frenchmen being driven out of their country for religion, have set foot in there; though afterwards again they have abandoned it.

What the Portuguese do at this day in Brazil, I know not; but it is likely now, that whatsoever there is held by the Christians, is reputed to be under the Spaniards, as many other parts of Brazil promiscuously are. Yet certain it is, that now almost 40 years since, some of the Frenchmen who practised sincere religion [Huguenots] and could not then be suffered quietly to live in France, did provide certain shipping under the conduct of one Villagagno[141] a Knight of Malta, but one of their own countrymen. They did go there, and continued there for the space of one year, having ministers and preachers amongst them, and the exercise of the Word and the sacraments. But afterwards, by the evil council of some of the chief rulers of France, who were addicted to the Pope, the heart of Villagagno was drawn away, in so much that he, insolently using the pastors and chiefs of that company, did force them to retire into France, so that the habitation there was then utterly relinquished, and has not since been continued by any of the French.

One who was in their voyage and has written a Tract, called *The Voyage to Brazil*, which is very well worth the reading, not only to see what did befall him and his company, but what the manners of that people and with whom they did converse. The inhabitants here are men also utterly unlearned, but men more ingenious then the common sort of the Americans. They are goodly of body, and straight of proportion, going always naked, reasonable good warriors after their country fashion, fattening up such enemies as they take in the wars, that afterwards they may devour them, which they do with great pleasure. For amongst some of the people of those quarters almost all are eaters of man's flesh.

In this country grows abundance of that wood which since is

---

[141] Nicolas de Villegagnon (1510-1571) invaded what is now Rio de Janeiro with a party of French Huguenots and Swiss Calvinists who sought to escape Catholic persecution at home. Abbot is less than fair to Villegagnon; the settlement failed after a Portuguese attack in 1558.

brought into Europe, to dye red colours, and is of the place where it comes called Brazil wood, the trees whereof are exceeding great.

From a description of the qualities of the people of Brazil where the French settlers lived, many things may be learned concerning the rest of the inhabitants near there about.

First then, they have no letters among them, and yet seem to be very capable of any good understanding: as appeared by the speech of some of them, reproving the Frenchmen for their great greediness and covetousness of gain, when they would take so much pains, as to come from another end of the world to get commodities there.

Their computation is only by the sun and moon, which they hold to be of a divine nature: and although they know nothing truly concerning God, yet they have a dark opinion that the soul does live after the separation from the body.

The men and women throughout the whole country do go stark naked, even very few of them having anything on to cover their privities, only some of them do pull some kind of ornaments through their ears, and the most of them have their lower lip bored through with a great hole, therein putting some device or other.

They are all wonderful straight of limb and proportion, insomuch that the author writes, that in all the time wherein he lived among them, he saw not one crooked back or any misshapen in any part: whereof seeking to give a reason, he ascribed it to this, that their children are never swathed nor bound about with anything when they are first born, but are put naked into the bed with their parents to lie; which beds are devised of cotton wool, and hung up between two trees not far from the ground, in the which flagging down in the middle, men and their wives and their children do lie together.

But whether this be the true reason of the straightness of their bodies, it may be doubted, from the authority of St Jerome, who in one of his treatises, mentioning that the children of the noblest and greatest Romans in his time, were very crooked, when others which were bred of meaner parents were not so, gives it this cause, that the gentlewomen of Rome, in a kind of wantonness, did not suffer their infants to be so long swathed as poorer people did, and that thereby their joints and members not being tied and restrained within compass, did fly out of proportion.

Certainly howsoever there may be some reasons naturally given of these things, it is much to be ascribed to the immediate will of God, who gives and takes away beauty at his pleasure.

The men of these parts are very strong, and able of body, and therefore either give sound strokes with their clubs wherewith they fight, or else shoot strongly with their bows, whereof they have plenty. If any of them be taken in the wars (after they have been crammed of purpose to be eaten of their enemies) they are brought forth to execution, wherein marvellous willingly they do yield themselves to death, as supposing that nothing can be more honourable to them, then to be taken, and to die for their country.

He therefore who is to kill the other, does with very much insolency and pride insult over him, which is to be slain; saying, "Thou art he who would have spoiled and destroyed us and ours, but now I am to recompense you for your pains." The other without all fear replies, "Yes, I am he that would have done it, and would spared none, if I had prospered in mine intent", and other such suitable words, showing their resolution to conquer, or willingly to die in the common cause of themselves and their people.

It is strange to see the inhumane and unnatural custom which many of the people of the West Indies have, for there are whole islands full of such cannibals as do eat man's flesh; when they are disposed to have any great meeting or to have any solemn feast, they kill some of their adversaries whom they keep in store for the purpose, and cut them out into collops [slices of meat], which they call boucan[142]. They will lay them upon the coals, and for several days together make great mirth in devouring them: wherein they

---

[142] More generally, boucan is used to mean smoked meat, or the grill on which it is smoked.

have this fashion, very strange, that so long as they are in their eating banquet, although it continue for days, they do never drink at all, but afterwards, when they are disposed to fall to drinking of a certain liquor which they have amongst them, they will continue boozing at it for two or three whole days, and in the meantime never eat.

In many parts both of New Spain and Peru, as also in the islands near adjoining, they have a herb, whereof they make great use; of which some is brought into divers parts of Europe, under the name of tobacco, although we have also much counterfeit of the same.

The people of those parts do use it as physic to purge themselves of humours, and they apply it also to the filling of themselves, the smoke of it being received through a leaf, or some such hollow thing, into the nostrils, head and stomach, and causing the party which receives, to lie as if he were drunk or dead for a space, needing no food or nourishment in the meanwhile.

Whereof it cannot be denied, but that it is possible that by prescription it may be serviceable for some purposes among us, although that is also very disputable, inasmuch as they who speak most highly of it, must and do confess that the force of it is stupefying and nothing else. Wise men should be wary and sparing in receiving of such a thing.

But when we do consider the vain and wanton use which many of our countrymen have of late taken up in receiving of this tobacco, not only many times in a day, but even at meat, and by the way to the great waste both of their purse and of their bodies, we may well deplore the vanity of the nation, who thereby propose themselves as ridiculous to the French, and other of our neighbours. And certainly, if it were possible that our worthy, warlike, and valiant progenitors, might behold the manners of those who do most delight therein they would wonder what a generation had succeeded in their place, who addict themselves to so fond, and worse than effeminate, passion[143].

Whosoever looks into those books, which our Christians travelling there have written, concerning those West Indies, shall find that the inhabitants there, do use it most as a remedy against syphilis, whereunto many of them are subject, being unclean in their associations; and that not only in fornication and adultery with women, but also their detestable and execrable sin of sodomy.

After that the Spaniards had for a time possessed New Spain, some of them travelled, toward the south for the desire of gold and pearl. By water they found the sea westward from Peru, which is always very calm, and is by them called the south sea, as the other, wherein Cuba stands, is termed the north sea, so by land they found that huge and mighty country, which is called Peru, wherein the people are (for the most part) very barbarous, and without God. Men of great stature, yes, some of them far higher than the ordinary sort of men in Europe, shooting strongly with bows made of fish bones, and most cruel people to their enemies.

Our English people who have travelled that way, do in their writings confess that they saw upon the south of Peru very huge and tall men, who advancing upon them when they put to land for fresh water, were much frightened with their guns, or else doubtless they had offered violence to them; which our men fearing, got themselves away as speedily as they could.

There was one Petrus de Cieca, a Spaniard, who when he had travelled 22 years, returned back again into Europe, and wrote an excellent book of the discovery of that whole country [*Chronica del Peru* (1554)]. And he amongst other things does record, that there are found in some parts of Peru, very huge and mighty bones of men that had been giants, who dwelt and were buried there.

Amongst these the Spaniards (partly by force but especially by

---

[143] Abbot's royal patron, James I, was the author in 1604 of *A Counterblaste to Tobacco,* where he refers to the habit as "A custom loathsome to the eye, hateful to the nose, harmful to the brain, dangerous to the lungs, and in the black stinking fume thereof, nearest resembling the horrible Stygian smoke of the pit that is bottomless".

perfidious treason) did get infinite sums of gold and pearls, wherewith being allured, they hoped for more, by reason that a great part thereof lies in the Tropics, and that caused them to spread themselves here, and there, as far as they durst in the country, where in some places they dug gold out of the earth; and in some other they found it ready dug and tried to their hands by the people of the country, which had used that trade before their coming there.

Among other creatures which are very famous in this Peru, there is a little beast called cincia[144], which is not bigger than a fox, the tail whereof is long, the feet short and the head like a very fox, which has a bag hanging under her belly, whereinto she does use to put her young, when she sees them in danger of any hunter or passenger.

That Petrus de Cieca (of whom mention was made before) tells that himself saw one of them, which had no less than seven young ones lying about her: but as soon as she perceived that a man was coming near to her, she presently got them into her bag, and ran away with such incredible swiftness as one would not have imagined.

After the Spaniards had conquered Mexico, travelling towards the south they discovered Peru, and just as they had prevailed against the Mexicans, by taking part with an enemy neighbour, so finding two brothers, Huáscar and Atahualpa, striving against each other in Peru, they contrived to ruin both of them, and got their incredible store of gold.

The first that attempted against the Peruvians and destroyed their Kings, were Diego de Almagro [1475-1538], Francisco Pizarro [1476-1541] and Pizarro's two brothers: but dealing treacherously and cruelly with the Peruvians, they enjoyed not long their victory, but all of them died a violent death.

The people of Peru are in many respects much wiser than those of Cuba, Hispaniola, and some other parts of the continent where

---

[144] Possibly based on erroneous impressions of chinchillas, whose defensive tactics include releasing their fur if bitten.

the Spaniards first landed, and therefore they have some orders and solemn customs among them; such as, among the rest, they bury their dead with ceremony, laying up their bodies with great solemnity into a large house prepared for that purpose.

They have also in one Province there a custom of carrying of news and messages very speedily, to the end that the King and Governor of the country may quickly be aware of anything which falls out; and this is not on horseback, or by the dromedary, as they use in other places, but only men who pass over rocks and through bushes the most direct way; and in certain set places there be always fresh runners to carry that farther which is brought to them by the other.

The Spaniards have here and there scatteringly upon the sea coasts set up some towns and castles but are not able to possess almost anything of the land: neither have they as yet discovered the inward parts thereof, though daily they spread themselves more and more. Insomuch that it is supposed that within these seven years last past, they have got into Guyana, where in former time no strength of that nation has been.

Guyana is a country which lies to the north in the same height as Peru to the south, about five degrees from the Equator, and that (as I take it) towards the south.

The country is supposed to be exceeding rich, and to have in it many mines of gold, which have not yet been touched, or at least but very lately, and are exceeding fertile; and delightful otherwise, although it lie in the heat of the tropics. There is such store of rivers and fresh waters in every part thereof, and the soil itself has such correspondency thereunto, that it reported to be as green and pleasant to the eye, as any place in the world.

Some of our Englishmen did with great labour and danger, pass by water into the heart of the country and earnestly desired that some forces of the English might be sent there, and a colony erected there. But by reason of the distance of the place and the great hazard, that if it should not succeed well it might prove dishonourable to our nation, and also because the Spaniards have great companies and strength, although not in it, yet many ways about it, that intendment was discontinued.

In parts of this Peru and Guyana there are very many great rivers, which as they are fit for any navigation that should be attempted to go up within the land, so otherwise they must needs yield health and fruitfulness to those that inhabit there. The greatest of these rivers is the Amazon River and next, down towards Magellan's straits, is the River Plate, and our Englishmen do speak of the river Orinoco. These are famed because for a good space after they have run into the main sea, yes, some write 20 or 30 miles, they keep themselves unmixed with the salt water, so that a very great way within the sea, men may take up as fresh water, as if they were near the land.

The first of our nation that sailed to Guyana, and made report thereof to us, was Sir Walter Raleigh, who travelled far up into the country upon the River Orinoco[145]. After him, one or two voyages there did Captain Keymis make, and now lately Captain Harcourt, with others, has visited that country, where our men continued the space of three or four years, being kindly treated by the natives, who much desire them to come and make some settlement amongst them, hoping by them to be defended against the Spaniards, whom they greatly hate and fear. When Sir Walter Raleigh came to Guyana he overthrew the Spaniards that were in Trinidad, and took Berrio their Captain or General, prisoner: he loosed and set at liberty four or five kings of the people of that country, that Berrio kept in chains, and sent them home to their own. Which deed of his did win him the hearts of that people, and make them much to favour our English at this day.

Divers also of that country, amongst them men of note, have been brought over into England, and here living many years, are by our men brought home to their own country; whose reports and knowledge of our nation is a cause that they have been well treated by these Guyanans, and much desired to settle themselves among

---

[145] In 1595, in the hope of finding the mythical Eldorado, the City of Gold.

them.

Our men that travelled to Guyana, amongst other things most memorable, did report, and in writing, delivered to the World, that near to Guyana, and not far from those places, where themselves were, there were men without heads, which seems to maintain the opinion to be true which in old time was conceived by the historians and philosophers, that there were those whose eyes were in their breasts, and the rest of their face there also situated. This our English travellers have reported to be so ordinarily and confidently mentioned, to them in those parts where they were, that no sober man should any way doubt of the truth thereof.

Now because it may appear that the matter is but fabulous, in respect of the truth of God's creating of them, and that the opinion of such strange shapes and monsters as were said to be in old time, that is, men with heads like dogs, some with ears down to their ankles, other with one huge foot alone, whereupon they did hop from place to place, was not worthy to be credited, it is fit that the certainty of the matter concerning these in Peru, should be known. And that is, that in some parts of Peru, the men are born as in other places, and yet by devices which they have, after the birth of children, when their bones and gristles, and other parts are yet tender and fit to be fashioned, they do crush down the heads of the children to the breasts and shoulders, and do with frames of wood and other such devices, keep them there, that in time they grow continuate to the upper part of the trunk of the body, and so seem to have no necks or heads. And again, some other of them thinking that the shape of the head is very decent, if it be long and erect after the fashion of a sugar loaf, do frame some other to that form by such wooden instruments, as they have for the purpose, and by binding and swathing them to keep them so afterwards. And that this is the custom of those people, Petrus de Cieca, who travelled almost all over Peru, and is a grave and sober writer, in his description of those countries, does report.

There be in some parts of Peru, people which have a strange device for the catching of divers sorts of fowls, wherein they especially desire to take such as have their feathers of pied, orient, and various colours, and that not so much for the flesh of them, which they may eat, as for their feathers, whereof they make garments, either short, as cloaks, or as gowns, long to the ground, and those their greatest nobles do wear, being curiously wrought, and by order, as appears by some of them being brought into England.

And here it is not amiss to specify, that in the sea, which is the ocean lying between Europe and America, there are flying fishes, yet whose wings are not feathers, but a thin kind of skin, like the wings of a bat or rear mouse. These, living sometimes in the water, and flying sometimes in the air, are well accepted in neither place, for below, either ravenous fishes are ready to devour them or above, the sea fowls are continually beating at them.

Some of the Spaniards desirous to see how far this land of Peru did go towards the south, travelled down, until at length they found the land's end, and a little strait or narrow sea, which did run from the main ocean towards Africa into the south sea. Magellan was he that found this dangerous strait, and passed through it, so that after him they are called the Straits of Magellan.

And this is the way whereby the Spaniards do pass to the backside of Peru, and New Spain and whosoever will compass the whole world (as some of our Englishmen have done) he must of necessity (for anything that is yet known) pass through this narrow strait. Ferdinand Magellan, having a great mind to travel, and being very desirous to go to the Moluccas by some other way, then by the backside of Africa if it might be, did in the year 1520 set forth from Seville in Spain with five ships and travelled toward the West Indies. He went so far towards the south as that he came to the land's end, where he, holding his course, in a narrow passage towards the west, for several days, did at length peaceably pass through the Straits, and came into a great sea which some name the Pacific Sea, because of the great calms and quietness of the waters there. But most commonly it is termed the South Sea, the length whereof he passed in the space of three months and 20 days, and came to the Moluccas, where being set upon by the people, himself and many of this company were slain. Yet one of his ships, the Victoria, did get away from those parts and returning by the Cape of Good Hope on the south side of Africa came safe to Spain.

So that it may be truly said, that if not Magellan, yet some of his company, were the first that did ever encompass the World through all the degrees of longitude.

The maps which were made at first concerning America and Peru described the western part of Peru as if when a man had passed Magellan's Straits, intending to come upward towards New Spain on the further side, he would have to bear much west, because the land shot out with a very great promontory, bending that way.

But our Englishmen who went with Sir Francis Drake did by their own experience certainly find that the land from the uttermost end of the Straights on the Peru side, did go up towards the south [perhaps north] directly, without bending to the west, and that is the cause wherefore all the new maps and globes, especially made by the English, or by the Dutch who have taken their directions from our men, are reformed according to this new observation.

When the Spaniards had once found an ordinary passage from the south sea towards the Moluccas, they never ceased to travel that way and discovered more and more: and by that means they have found out divers Islands not known in former ages; as two for example sake, a good distance from the Moluccas which because they be inhabited by men which do steal not only each from other, but do pilfer away all things that they can from such strangers as do land thereabouts, they are called The Island of Thieves.

They have also described some other nearer to the East Indies, which they now term the Solomon Islands. But the most renowned of all, are those of whom the name is given the Philippines, in remembrance of Philip II, King of Spain, at whose cost they were discovered.

These Philippines are very rich, and from there is brought abundance of costly spices, and some other rich merchandise; yes, and gold too.

There were also some other Islands described by Magellan himself, which he called *The Unfortunate Islands*[146] as being of quality contrary to the Canaries, which are termed *The Fortunate Islands*: for when he passing through the south sea, and meaning to come to the Moluccas, (where he was slain)[147] did land in these islands thinking there to have furnished himself with victuals, and fresh water, he found the whole places to be barren, and not inhabited.

---

[146] About the location, and very existence, of which there is some debate but few conclusions.

[147] Magellan was in fact slain in the Philippines – which may be what Abbot has in mind in this and the next section in some cases when he refers to the Moluccas.

Of the Countries that lie about the two Poles

Having laid down in some measure the description of the old known world, Asia, Africa and Europe, with the islands adjoining to them and also of America, which by some has the title of New-found-World: it shall not be amiss briefly to say something of a fifth and sixth part of the earth, the one lying near the South Pole, and the other near the North, which are places that in former times were not known, nor thought of.

When Magellan was come down to the southern end of Peru, he found on the further side of the Straits a main and huge land lying towards the South Pole, which some have from his name called the Kingdom of Magellan, the more so because he touched upon it again before he came to the Moluccas.

Since his time, Portuguese, trading towards the East Indies, have some of them been driven by tempest so far, as to that which many now call the South Continent, and so many men of sundry nations have there by occasion touched upon it.

It is found therefore by experience, for to go along all the degrees of longitude, and as in some places, it is certainly discovered to come up so high towards the north, as to the Tropic of Capricorn. So it is conjectured, that towards the south it goes as far as to the Pole. The ground whereof is, that never any man did perceive the sea did pass through any part thereof: no, there is not any great river which has yet been described to come out of it into the ocean. Whereupon it is concluded that since somewhat must fill up the globe of the earth from the first appearing of this land to the very Pole: and that cannot be any sea, unless it should be such a one as has no intercourse with the ocean (which to imagine is uncertain) therefore it is supposed that it comes whole out into the land to the Antarctic Pole. If this be granted, it must needs be acknowledged withal that this space of earth is so huge, as that it equals in greatness not only Asia, Europe and Africa, but almost America, being joined to them.

Things memorable in this country are yet reported to be very few, only in the east part of over against the Moluccas. Some have written that there be very waste countries and wildernesses, but we find not so much as mention whether any do inhabit there or not. And over against the promontory of Africa which is called the Cape of Good Hope, there is a country which the Portuguese called *Land of Parrots*, because of the abundant store of parrots which they found there.

Near to Magellan's Straits in this south part of the world, is that land the Spaniards call *Tierra Del Fuego* [the land of fire]; those also which have touched at it in other places, have given to some parts of it these names, Beach, Lucach, and Maletur, but we have no perfect description of it, nor any knowledge how or by whom it is inhabited.

About this place, the said Portuguese did at one time sail along for the space of 2000 miles and yet found no end of the land. And in this place, they reported that the saw inhabitants, which were very fair and fat people, and did go naked: which is the more to be observed because we scant read in any writer, that there has been seen any people at all upon the south coast.

More towards the east, not far from the Moluccas, there is one part of this country, as some suppose, although some doubt whether that be an Island or not, which comes up so high towards the north, as the very equatorial line, and this is commonly called New Guinea, because it lies in the same climate, and is of no other temperature than Guinea in Africa is.

I have heard a great mathematician in, find fault with all our late makers of maps, because in describing this continent, they make no mention of any cities, kingdoms, or commonwealth which are seated and placed there: whereof he seemed in confidence of words to avouch, that there be a great many, and that it is as good a country as almost any in the world. But the arguments why he gathered it to be so he did not deliver; and yet notwithstanding, it may be the most probably conjectured, that the Creator of World would not have framed so huge a mass of earth, but that he would in his wisdom appoint some reasonable creatures to have their habitation there.

Concerning those places which may be supposed to lie near to the Northern Pole, there has in times past something been written, which for the particularity thereof might carry some show of truth, if it be not thoroughly looked into. It is therefore by an old tradition delivered, and by some written also, that there was a friar of Oxford[148], who took on him to travel into those parts, which are under the very Pole, which he did partly by necromancy (wherein he was much skilled) and partly again by taking advantage of the frozen times, by means whereof he might travel upon the ice even so as himself pleased. It is said therefore of him, that he was directly under the Pole, and that there he found a very huge and black rock, and that the said rock, being divers miles in circuit, is compassed round about with the sea. Which sea, being the breadth of some miles over, does run out into the more large ocean by four several currents, which is as much to say, as that a good pretty way distant from that rock, there are four several lands of reasonable quantity, and being situated round about the rock, although with some good distance, are severed each from other by the sea running between them, and making them all four to be islands almost of equal bigness. But there is no certainty of this report, and therefore our best mathematicians in this latter age have omitted it.

Our travellers of later years have adventured so far, to their great danger, in those cold and frozen countries, that they have described Greenland; which lies as far or beyond the Arctic Circle. But whether it goes so far out as to the Pole, they cannot say: which is also to be affirmed of the northern parts of America, for the opening whereof our Englishmen have taken great pains, as may easily appear by the new globes and maps, in which all the capes, sounds and furlongs, are called by English names. Their purpose

---

[148] The unknown author of a lost 14th century book, *Inventio Fortunata* (= *The Lucky Discovery*)

was in attempting this voyage, to have found out a passage to China and Cathay by the north parts of America. But by the snows which fell in August and September, as also by the incredible ice there, after many hazards of their lives, they were forced to return, not knowing whether there be any current of the sea, that might lead to the East Indies, or how far the land does reach northward.

In like sort, some of our English Merchants have to their great charges set forth fleets to descry the seas towards the east, yet going by the north, and there have found many unknown countries, as Novaya Zemlya, Sir Hugh Willoughby's land and other more: but what is very near to the Pole, they could never find. They have also so far prevailed, as to reach one half of the way towards Cathay by the north, going eastwards: in so much that by the River Ob, and by the Bay of Saint Nicholas, they bring the merchandise downward into Russia. But whether the sea goes throughout, even to the farthest eastern parts, or whether some great promontory stretches out of the main continent to the very Pole, they cannot yet attain to know. These things therefore must be left uncertain, to further discoveries in future ages.

info@goldenford.co.uk
www.goldenford.co.uk